P9-DWJ-928

PATTERNS OF POLITY

PATTERNS OF POLITY

VARIETIES OF CHURCH GOVERNANCE

EDWARD LeROY LONG, JR.

THE
PILGRIM
PRESS
Cleveland

The Pilgrim Press, 700 Prospect Avenue E.,
Cleveland, Ohio 44115-1100, U.S.A.
www.pilgrimpress.com

© 2001 by Edward LeRoy Long, Jr.

All rights reserved. Published 2001

Printed in the United States of America on acid-free paper

06 05 04 03 02 01   5 4 3 2 1

Library of Congress Cataloging-in-Publication Data
Long, Edward LeRoy.
    Patterns of polity : varieties of church governance / Edward LeRoy
Long, Jr.
        p.   cm.
    Includes bibliographical references and index.
    ISBN 0-8298-1444-2 (pbk. : alk. paper)
    1. Church polity. 2. Church management.   I. Title.
BV650 .L66 2001
262 – dc21

                                                        2001034043

Contents

Prologue

T HIS BOOK IS WRITTEN out of the conviction that much can be learned from a comparative examination of the widely different patterns of governance found in contemporary branches of Christianity. The aim of such an overview is not to legitimate a particular polity on scriptural or historical grounds, and certainly not to discredit any particular polity, but rather to understand how different ways of governing affairs affect decision making within various Christian groups. Understanding how different polities work can greatly enhance the awareness of how the polity with which we are familiar compares with those of other Christians. We understand ourselves by noting how we differ from others as much as by knowing how we function ourselves. A knowledge of comparative polities may also be helpful in advancing covenantal cooperation among Christian groups, since such cooperation necessarily must take into account how different polities can function in relationship to each other.

The premises that inform this overview differ in some respects from some long-standing assumptions about the origins and significance of denominationalism. More than seven decades ago, H. Richard Niebuhr drew attention to the cultural and political roots of the divisions in American church life.[1] Niebuhr was concerned with the distinguishing features of particular groups, a great many of which he argued were created by cultural and political influences rather than explicitly theological considerations. While this observation may be especially true of the creation of denominational divisions, and may have carried over to some extent into the present life of various churches, much has happened to make the correlation between denominational identity and social class less clear than when Niebuhr wrote. Today it may be

---

1. H. Richard Niebuhr, *The Social Sources of Denominationalism* (New York: Henry Holt, 1929).

just as plausible to examine denominational influences on social behavior (or at least on the behavior and expectation of members) as to emphasize the social sources of church identities. The movement between culture and church does not take place in only one direction.

More recently, the phrase "post-denominational" has come to be used with considerable frequency. Sociologists like Robert Wuthnow, Rodney Stark, and Charles Glock have been suggesting that denominational differences no longer matter very much.[2] People—at least those with moderate outlooks on religious matters—seem able to move casually from one tradition to another without sensing major differences. Moreover, denominational identity has given way to categories like the religious right and the religious left. People may choose to affiliate with a local church because it represents one of these poles rather than because it is connected with a particular denomination. Many denominations are currently caught in a cleavage between conservative and liberal perspectives, which often makes the differences within denominations as great as the differences between them. However, that cleavage has not done away with differences in governance. Polity still affects how denominations function, even if many denominations are dealing with the same issues in somewhat different ways.[3]

Despite the importance of governance for understanding the churches in all their institutional diversity, most theological education ordinarily focuses attention on the study of doctrine. The usual seminary curriculum treats the polity course as a matter of logistical or operational concern—something necessary professionally but not intellectually important. The course in polity is usually taken (sometimes begrudgingly) to qualify for a leadership position within one specific denominational or ecclesiastical

---

2. This theme is explored in Robert Wuthnow, *The Restructuring of American Religion: Society and Faith since World War II* (Princeton, N.J.: Princeton University Press, 1988), and Rodney Stark and Charles Y. Glock, *Patterns of Religious Commitment* (Berkeley: University of California Press, 1988).

3. For a series of essays indicating the continuing importance of understanding denominational identities, see Robert Bruce Mullin and Russell F. Richey, eds., *Reimagining Denominationalism: Interpretive Essays* (New York and Oxford: Oxford University Press, 1994).

group. But if it is true that patterns of governance determine how ecclesiastical systems work, a far better understanding of churches as institutions can come from increased awareness of the forms of governance and of the logistical and ethical problems that arise within ecclesiastical groups by virtue of the ways they are governed. Understanding polity should not be merely an exercise in parochialism but a fundamental branch of theological study that can provide the depth and breadth of understanding necessary to deal with vexing issues in ecumenical cooperation. The study of polity should be an intriguing exploration of fundamental theoretical and functional differences.

Perhaps it is because the study of polity is often peripheral and parochial that church controversies are especially intractable (and occasionally heated), especially when cooperation is attempted between churches having different views as to how Christian groups should be governed. Efforts to create working relationships among mainline churches frequently flounder, not so much over differences about doctrine, but over differences about governance. Problems arise because the differences in governance have not been carefully explored and adequately understood, and there is insufficient appreciation within one group of how governance functions in other groups. It may be that failures in this area occur because members of one church do not have adequate understandings of governance patterns of other churches. They react negatively (with a jerk of the knee, so to speak) to generalized impressions about governance patterns other than their own rather than out of an emphatic and well-informed understanding of how such patterns actually work.

Attention to doctrine, to the eclipse of broad understandings of polity, creates one kind of problem in the understanding of the life and work of churches. Another set of problems comes from the tendency of ethicists to focus on the moral issues found outside church life. In the World Council of Churches, the branch that focuses on the nature of churches has historically been identified by the rubric "faith and order." This terminology refers both to doctrine and governance. The other branch, conducted under the rubric of "life and work," has focused on the programs and activities of churches and on the outreach of churches to the world. It is often assumed that ethicists are primarily concerned with "life and work," leaving "faith and order" to theologians and church bureaucrats. To be sure, specific matters of ecclesiastical order have occasionally been examined by ethicists, and some social theorists have paid attention to ecclesiastical forms of institutional life. But the numerous ethical issues that can arise in ecclesiastical affairs have not been addressed as fully or as systematically by theological ethicists as the ethical problems posed by other social institutions. In short, Christian social ethicists have often been more concerned about the behavior of social institutions other than those within which many of them work.[4]

Although this book will not explore every ethical issue posed by governance in ecclesiastical bodies, it will identify the kinds of issues most likely to arise under each pattern of governance discussed. Such examination includes questions like, In what ways is power created and used in different polities? What do different polities do best and in what matters do they function worst? In what ways are polities most likely to become corrupt? Whose interests are they most likely to serve? How are conflicts adjudicated? How are property and finances handled?

The importance of understanding the various ways in which churches are governed was explicitly affirmed in the *Report of the Eighteenth Plenary of the Consultation on Church Union,* resulting from the St. Louis gathering in January 1999. This report suggests, among other activities designed to foster greater understanding among constituent churches, "that the history, theology, and polity of all the participating churches be taught in our seminaries and that candidates for ministry show knowledge of the other churches."[5]

Such comparative study is done rarely, if at all, even in nondenominational seminaries in which the student body comes from

---

4. The division between "faith and order" and "life and work" is slowly being transcended in recent ecumenical endeavors, especially in studies of the relationship between ecclesiology and ethics that have engaged several Christian ethicists. For an example of recent thinking that transcends the division and that offers a guide to the deliberations and emerging literature, see Lewis S. Mudge, *The Church as Moral Community: Ecclesiology and Ethics in Ecumenical Debate* (New York: Continuum; Geneva: WCC Publications, 1998).

5. Available at http://www.cocu.org/cocu/cocurepo.html. The recommendation cited comes from section 7.

many traditions. Although existing materials in church history and theology may be helpful for this inquiry, the suggestion by the Consultation on Church Union (COCU) calls for new resources—studies that can facilitate instruction concerning polities and the implications of polities on the life of Christian groups. Such study need not be confined to the mainline churches involved in COCU, since they can learn, not only from each other, but from the variations in patterns of governance that have arisen among other Christian movements. After all, were several mainline Christian denominations to forge a high degree of covenantal togetherness, they would still not constitute the whole of Christendom. Many groups would remain, both the highly traditional and highly innovative, indicating that Christianity has spawned widespread and diverse movements—all believing that they conduct their affairs in faithful obedience to the gospel.

I wish to express my appreciation to many persons who have helped to bring this book into being. Most numerous are the unnamed, who have kept me going by saying in several ways, "A book like this is needed!" Then there are those who have responded to the draft of the chapter or section that deals with the polity with which they are familiar: Charles Curran, Stanley Harakas, Gene Kraus, Timothy Sedgwick, Andy Smith, Timothy Staveteig, Edgar Towne, and D. Newell Williams. Three friends, William Saum, James Smylie, and Charles Yrigoyen, read the entire draft and offered both encouragement and helpful observations. The libraries at Union Theological Seminary in Virginia and Drew University offered service beyond the normal practice. My wife, Dr. Grace Cumming Long, helped in preparing the manuscript for submission and by enduring my preoccupation with the project during its slow emergence. I was greatly helped by the superb editorial work done on this book under the direction of George Graham of Pilgrim Press, and by the remarkable editorial and design skills of John Eagleson.

Introduction

EXPLORING POLITIES TO UNDERSTAND FAITH TRADITIONS

THIS IS A BOOK about how churches are governed. Normally, in thinking about various Christian groups, less attention is given to their governance than to their beliefs. For instance, in the monumental study of religious bodies written by Arthur Carl Piepkorn, under the title *Profiles in Belief,*[1] the distinguishing beliefs of various groups are described, together with the historical background of the different ecclesial bodies, but less is said about their governance.

To be sure, beliefs are important and often help to shape the nature of the institutions in which they are held. Identifying beliefs are usually embodied in creeds—formally adopted statements of doctrinal belief that constitute the core convictions of a particular group. Creeds do furnish one clue to the nature of particular churches or church groups, but there are only a few churches— for example, Unitarians—whose beliefs stand out so sharply from other groups as to cause their doctrinal position to be the reason for their names. Although there may be particular beliefs associated with different Christian groupings—such as predestination associated with the Reformed tradition, moral earnestness with holiness groups, and believer's baptism with the Baptists— the doctrinal positions of most mainline denominations are quite similar. Even their disagreements about matters of faith and morals are similar. But their polities are different.

---

1. *Profiles in Belief: The Religious Bodies of the United States and Canada,* vol. 1: *Roman Catholic, Old Catholic, and Eastern Orthodoxy;* vol. 2: *Protestant Denominations;* vol. 3: *Holiness and Pentecostal;* vol. 4: *Evangelical, Fundamentalist, and Other Christian Bodies* (New York: Harper and Row, 1977–79).

1

Beliefs about Governance

It is true that churches believe certain things about governance as well as about doctrinal matters. These governance patterns deserve to be better understood, for differences and contrasts among mainline church groups may be seen more clearly by comparing governance than by comparing doctrines. There are clear and abiding differences in the patterns of governance— generally called the "polities"—of different churches. Several of the major denominations carry names that point to the procedures by which they govern their affairs (for example, *Episcopalian* for groups that govern with bishops; *Presbyterian* for churches that govern with elders; and *Congregationalist* for groups that place authority in the local membership). This means that governance may be at least as important as creeds in understanding denominations.

Polity provides institutional cohesion to many groups. Many denominations manage to stay intact despite cleavages in doctrine, unresolved differences in moral positions, and debates about social attitudes. They probably would not stay intact if equally divisive controversy existed about matters of governance and procedure. The so-called right and left in a denomination may bitterly disagree about a theological judgment or social witness but are generally loyal to the same polity, though they may well argue about the decisions by that polity.

In thinking about one group's polity, it is important to begin with that group's definition of its nature and purpose. How does it define its reason for being? A group may express its reasons for being in various ways. It may do so with creedal statements, and it may do so in constitutions—particularly in preambles (or prefaces) to such instruments. It may express its reason for being in covenants of purpose that supplement constitutions and that are frequently drawn up by local divisions of the denomination, rather than by its major governing body. Although such statements are important clues to a group's purposes, such groups seldom exist merely to hold certain beliefs; they usually exist to do certain things. The way groups do things frequently receives direction from polity, which reveals how a group believes things should be done. Procedures therefore become as significant as affirmations, polity as significant as doctrine.[2]

Constitutional Provisions and Living Processes

The governance of ecclesiastical institutions is a complex matter that defies description in simple categories. Although formal structure may be set forth in constitutional provisions, the constitutions of church groups vary widely in how, and the extent to which, they provide the definitive clue to the governance patterns of those groups. Some constitutions are detailed and explicit; others are general and leave much to inference and custom. Some are left to stand as originally written; others are constantly revised or amended as new occasions call for new responses.

Constitutional provisions cannot be ignored, but they do not necessarily reveal the living processes within particular groups. Just as it is necessary in the study of American government to read both the Constitution and the Supreme Court decisions that have interpreted the Constitution, it is necessary in dealing with ecclesiastical governance to know not only the statutes that formally define the polity, but also the decisions that have affected the character and practices of the group. The governance of any particular group may even have dimensions that go beyond the juridical processes and decisions that have taken place in its history. Even more important than the allegiance to constitutions and precedents are insights about how a group's ecclesial machinery works and into the many subtle factors that give a unique "feel" or "flavor" to its ethos—that is, to the quality of its communal being. This is especially true of churches, in contrast, for

---

2. In "Denominations: Who and What Are We Studying?" in *Reimagining Denominationalism: Interpretive Essays*, ed. Robert B. Mullin and Russell E. Richey (New York and Oxford: Oxford University Press, 1994), 111–33, Nancy T. Ammerman suggests that three factors must be considered in denominational studies: beliefs and practices; organizational structures; and cultural identities. While it is probably impossible to understand a religious group by any one of these factors, theologians likely have devoted more attention to the first and social scientists more to the third; the second factor has received the least attention. If this overview pays more attention to organizational structure than to the other two factors, it may help redress an imbalance rather than achieve an adequate perspective on the groups discussed.

instance, to political units. The "feel" or "flavor" is difficult to explain by examining the constitutional (or equivalent) instrument by which a group's governance is formally described or historically interpreted. The behavioral patterns of the community and the unofficial conventions that sustain and shape those patterns have to be considered in understanding how the polity functions. Polity in its broadest sense is a matter, not only of laws and juridical interpretations, but of conventions and community behavior. Sometimes even the members of a denomination are not fully aware how these subtle aspects affect them, which makes the effort to understand various church bodies almost daunting.

In order to understand ecclesiastical polities, therefore, we must look at the varied and complex set of factors that give any group its unique identity. Not every factor operates in every case, and the absence (or limited use) of any factor or group of factors may be as much a clue to the nature of the group as its presence. For instance, all groups have ways of determining membership. These can vary from the most restrictive requirements to open membership. Even a group that refuses to define membership requirements does not thereby cease to have a polity; it simply has a polity of claimed openness about this aspect of governance. By what processes are members inculturated into the group (by birth, by conversion, by instruction, by probationary participation, or a combination thereof)? Is there any initiation process or ritual passage in joining, and how extensive and how formal is it?

When thinking about membership it is important to know not only how admission takes place but what prompts people to belong. Does a group seek new members or discourage them? What expectations do the members have? What are the advantages and obligations of belonging? Are the conditions of membership met at entrance, or are conditions reviewed periodically and the standing of members reexamined?

The polity of a particular church group is often more congenial to persons with certain temperaments than to others. Some groups appeal to those with aesthetic bents; others to those with humanitarian passion; others to those who enjoy (or who can at least tolerate) parliamentary maneuvering; still others to those who find political interaction uncongenial and who are content to have decisions made for them. These factors become increasingly important as people become actively involved in a church group. Many people associate with local congregations for extraneous reasons that bear little or no relationship to polity. Many persons may simply join a church because casual attendance seems to show its appeal. However, a person cannot fully participate in a church without paying attention to its polity and ethos. And if a person assumes a leadership position there is no escape from having to reckon with the polity and how it operates.

Polity determines how rules and procedures are developed, sustained, and sanctioned. Although no polity is fixed and immutable, church groups cannot reinvent their procedures for every occasion. Although every polity undergoes developmental change—sometimes significantly—at any given time the polity usually determines how rules and procedures are enacted and/or enforced. Most polities provide for changes, not only changes in conformity with the ongoing polity, but sometimes changes in the polity itself. The provisions that a constitution makes for amendments to itself are a very important aspect of a polity. In some polities such changes can occur easily; in others, they are very difficult. Some of the greatest difficulties arise, not because the polity is clear and specific about making changes, but because the provisions are not spelled out and, hence, become matters of contention.

THE SIGNIFICANCE OF SYMBOLS

Groups frequently have symbols through which they point to their reason (or reasons) for being. Although creeds are sometimes referred to as symbols, many other devices that give a group its identity are determined by the polity, either directly or indirectly. The utilization of symbols contributes significantly to group ethos. Even if the group decries or repudiates the use of symbols, or at least the use of overt symbols, that suggests an ethos or polity characteristic rather than the absence of a polity. The absence of symbols does not necessarily mean they have no bearing on spirituality. Quakers and some of the Reformed bodies in Europe have made a powerful symbolism out of austerity—that is, out of the lack of symbols.

Liturgical events have symbolic significance. The observance of the Last Supper of Christ is present in most Christian groups, but the manner of its celebration and, more particularly, the symbolic role it occupies vary enormously. In some polities, the celebration of the Eucharist is carefully preserved as a function of the clergy; in others, the sacrament (or celebration) is done by laity, sometimes even without the clergy. Apart from the doctrinal interpretation given to this liturgical act, a set of meanings attaches to the celebration by the frequency (or infrequency) of its observation, by the provisions of the polity that define who can celebrate, and by the manner in which it observed. Some of the most scrupulous ways of celebrating this liturgical act are associated with groups that are rather loose in defining it doctrinally—though this is not always the case, and the converse can be true as well.

Attire, whether of clergy or of all group members, has important symbolic functions. Not only does it identify persons as belonging to the group or as exercising leadership, but clothing creates an aura, with powerful functional significance. Matters of attire differ from denomination to denomination (and sometimes even within a denomination). In some cases a particular practice is required; in other cases, it is optional. Such differences often create strong responses and overt controversies, especially when the practice differs within a denomination. Even the non-use of special attire gives a group its own feel or flavor.

MEMBERSHIP, CONFLICT, AND AUTHORITY

What provisions exist in the group for rendering care and nurture to members? There may be wide differences not only among different Christian groups but even between local congregations belonging to a denomination with the same polity. Nevertheless, polity does bear on pastoral care, particularly on whether churches assume the task of caring for the temporal as well as spiritual needs of their members, or whether the clergy alone are qualified to render certain services. There is also the question whether such care is primarily sacramental and formal, or therapeutic and personal.

Some of the groups in which mutual aid and support are practiced most fully provide that aid and support through laypersons rather than clergy.

In thinking about the forms and meaning of membership, it is necessary to ask about the possibility of alternative roles. Is there only one kind of belonging, or are there different levels (or orders) of membership? Are such differences related in a communal, complementary, or hierarchical fashion? How do members relate to the group and to each other? What roles do subgroups play? Are ad hoc groups encouraged or discouraged?

Polities also differ greatly in the extent to which conformity and obedience are expected. Some presuppose rigid conformity to the group's official beliefs or practices; others tolerate diversity and even encourage alternative patterns of fidelity as a desirable aspect of discipleship. While clearly defined and formally applied sanctions generally are associated with groups that have the most explicit rules and expect the greatest conformity to those rules, even this relationship has to be looked at on a case-by-case basis rather than as an inevitable function of any particular kind of formal governance. The judicatories that oversee individual congregations in a given district or convention can enforce the same polity in widely different ways. The existence of a rigid rule sometimes brings about a decision not to invoke it, whereas a looser polity can be become a matter of contention between parties as they seek to legitimize vindictive strategies aimed at driving out opposition. It is necessary to examine how groups deal with variances from polity, whether willful and explicit, or casual and unexpected (even unintended). When are such variations handled as pastoral concerns, and when are they handled as punishable offenses? These decisions may differ from instance to instance within the same polity. Although generalizations are therefore difficult to make, churches nevertheless develop histories that give clues as to how such matters are dealt with. Those histories have much to do with determining the nature of a religious group.

One of the important aspects of any polity is the provision for handling conflicts and disputes. Are there formal processes for resolving disputes, or are disputes handled in ways that politicize the issues? Do disputes persist until one side caves in? Will groups split when differences arise that cannot be resolved within the polity's processes? Are such splits likely to come about because one side is ousted or because one side withdraws? How does group polity determine the most likely result?

Behind several of the previous considerations lies the matter of authority. How is authority created in each of the polities? Do leaders function by fiat and/or domination, or by example and/or persuasion? What happens when authority is challenged? One source of authority stems from the loyalty of members. Authority can be maintained by threatening to oust, or by ousting, those who do not conform to the polity. This approach is effective only if members care about membership. Do the provisions for removing members yield slow and cumbersome decisions or quick and easy decisions? But ousting nonconformers may not be the primary pattern. Can churches handle ecclesiastical disobedience, and to what degree can the polity (or the ethos) allow membership among persons with sharply different views and practices?

What provisions in the polity, whether formally specified or adhered to as convention, specify the accountability of leaders? Many churches have procedures for measuring the performance and for monitoring the professionalism and spirituality of their leaders. In other polities, leaders develop their own ways of doing things. One of the differences, for instance, between Billy Graham and many other evangelists lies in this area. Graham believed in having an association monitor his activities, account for his monetary intake and outlays, and otherwise insure the responsible conduct of his affairs. This is not true of every publicly visible or individual evangelist, many of whom need answer only to themselves and who can operate without regard to the responsibilities that attend institutional definition.

Major Forms of Governance

The chapters that follow are arranged according to the three commonly acknowledged patterns of governance—*rule by bishops*, *rule by elders*, and *rule by congregational decisions*. Each pattern exists in a wide variety of forms, requiring separate chapters within each division. The nature of episcopacy, for instance, is very different in the polity and ethos of the Episcopal Church than in the polity and ethos of the Methodist tradition; eldership means something quite different in Presbyterian churches than among the Amish and the Quakers; congregationalism runs the gamut from connectionalism—approaching the interaction in the other major forms of governance—to completely autonomous groups. A bishop may or may not have significant power; elders may or may not be ruling officials; congregations may or may not be free to set their own rules and to define their own procedures. One of the curious facts about polity is the extent to which some of the same titles—such as "bishop" and "elder"—are used in polities for offices with different functions. Unless one has a clear sense of what a term means in one tradition there is a danger of misunderstanding that tradition.

All of these factors make the analysis of ecclesiastical polity complex. The chapters that follow do not use just one sequence in describing these many factors. Instead, the descriptions will, as much as possible, start with an exposition of features in a polity that provide its most distinctive character. Those qualities will then be clues by which to understand how other factors, as they are incorporated, are shaped.

Resources for Understanding the Nature of Polity

Dulles, Avery. *Models of the Church.* Garden City, N.Y.: Doubleday, 1974.

Mead, Frank S. *Handbook of Denominations in the United States.* Revised by Samuel S. Hill. New 10th ed. Nashville: Abingdon Press, 1995.

Mudge, Lewis S. *The Church as Moral Community: Ecclesiology and Ethics in Ecumenical Debate.* Geneva: WCC Publications; New York: Continuum, 1998.

Mullin, Robert Bruce, and Russell E. Richey, eds., *Reimagining Denominations: Interpretive Essays.* New York: Oxford University Press, 1994.

Niebuhr, H. Richard. *Social Sources of Denominationalism.* New York: Henry Holt, 1929.

Piepkorn, Arthur Carl. *Profiles in Belief: The Religious Bodies of the United States and Canada.* Vol. 1: *Roman Catholic, Old Catholic, and East-*

ern *Orthodoxy*. Vol. 2: *Protestant Denominations*. Vol. 3: *Holiness and Pentecostal*. Vol. 4: *Evangelical, Fundamentalist, and Other Christian Bodies*. New York: Harper and Row, 1977–79.

Reuver, Marc. *Faith and Law: Juridical Perspectives for the Ecumenical Movement*. Geneva: WCC Publications, 2000.

Schaver, J. L. *The Polity of the Churches*. Vol. 1: *Concerns All the Churches of Christendom*. Chicago: Church Polity Press, 1947.

Schwenk, Robert L., ed. *Constitutions of American Denominations*. Buffalo: William S. Hein, 1984.

Williams, J. Paul. *What Americans Believe and How They Worship*. Rev. ed. New York and Evanston, Ill.: Harper and Row, 1962.

Part One

GOVERNANCE BY BISHOPS

1

MONARCHICAL EPISCOPACY

A LTHOUGH THERE IS NO UNIFORM TERMINOLOGY for speaking about polities that depend on bishops, it is possible to speak of three major variations: *monarchical, managerial,* and *pastoral* forms of episcopacy. These terms distinguish among three patterns of governance that are different from one another, despite their common use of episcopal leadership. These terms should be understood in the context of church practice, even though some are borrowed from types of leadership in secular institutions.

For instance, *monarchical* is not used to mean dictatorial in a political sense; rather, it indicates that the functions of episcopacy are carried on by persons of immense symbolic stature, who bear full responsibility for maintaining the integrity of the church as an institution. *Managerial* is not used to signify control in a commercial sense or by virtue of ownership; rather, it indicates that the bishop uses clearly defined and officially delineated authority to see that an ecclesiastical organization functions with maximum effectiveness. And *pastoral* does not mean caring only for feelings of church members; rather, it means that the bishop facilitates the conduct of affairs within the church, primarily by means of nurture and persuasion.

All episcopacy has a hierarchical quality in the sense that bishops have long experience in the group they are chosen to lead. They occupy preeminence by virtue of their office, but this does not mean that all versions of episcopacy function by commands. It does mean that all versions of episcopacy focus on the maintenance of faith and order by placing respected and competent persons in a carefully defined and formally acknowledged position of leadership—however differently that leadership may be exercised.

GOVERNANCE IN THE ROMAN CATHOLIC CHURCH

The monarchical form of episcopacy is found in its clearest form in
the governance of the Roman Catholic Church. The term *monarchical* has been used since the time of Ignatius to designate an
episcopacy in which a single official (in Roman Catholicism, always a man) has responsibility to protect the faith, to preserve
right doctrine, and to supervise church life within a given district.
Although a monarchical bishop may delegate duties to subordinates, he bears sole responsibility for the governance of that area
(usually a geographical district) over which he is in charge. This
is called a *diocese.* All subordinate officials—which together constitute a bureaucracy—are subject to the direction and control of
the bishop, who may install or remove subordinates as he sees fit.

Although the leadership and influence of the bishop over his
own diocese are theoretically unilateral, such leadership is different from that of a political tyrant. The actions of every bishop are
governed by the doctrine and practices of the wider church as well
as by an extensive body of canon law. Under modern conditions,
moreover, the church cannot be a totalitarian regime because it
does not have the power to exercise authority over every aspect
of the social order, as dictatorships in the political sense attempt
to do. Even in countries in which a church governed monarchi-
cally has official standing within the state, time has long since
past when an ecclesiastical official can command behavior from
the unchurched. The official may not even be able to demand
conformity from the members of his own flock. Nevertheless, the
formal concept of this governance presupposes that subordinate
officials and ordinary church members will obey the instructions
of the bishop in all things that have to do with faith and morals,
whether these matters involve the internal affairs of the church
or their life as believers.

Moreover, in the Roman Church—in significant distinction
from the status that autonomous ruling monarchs might have
within nation-states—all bishops are subject to the restraints of
larger collegiums of which they are members. Such bodies gather
on both national and international levels. On the international
level, every bishop is a member of the College of Bishops, which

is headed by the pope. The actions of every bishop are guided by its policies.

THE ROLE OF THE POPE

The pope is the first bishop among bishops. His role cannot be understood as that of an official who sets policy at will and who gives orders to all other bishops, nor can it be understood as that of one who chairs a parliamentary process for making decisions. The pope is a monarchical bishop who can exercise the same supervisory power over the diocese of Rome that other bishops exercise in their own jurisdictions, but his role in the church as a whole rests on a complex mixture of religious agreement, shared tradition, respect, charisma, and voluntary allegiance rather than on a capacity to induce fear in underlings by threatening them with harm extrinsic to the system. Because the pope is a first among equals rather than a head over subordinates, it is misleading to think of the papacy as a dictatorship that wields arbitrary power, or as a corporation that controls all operations from headquarters. It is equally misleading to think of the pope as a parliamentary figure who presides over a group in which all policy-making activities are done collegially. According to Thomas J. Reese, "This role is a unique one, without any secular or religious counterparts, and it is not easily understood either inside or outside the Catholic church."[1]

The papacy derives its role from the governance of the Roman Church, not by using naked power to quash enemies (as dictators often attempt) but from the workings of a massive institutional process that has developed and been refined by many years of experience and achievement. Although, in the early church, bishops were probably elected by the apostolic community, the selection and installation of bishops now occurs by appointment. In some periods of Western history, the secular leader was able to influence the appointment of bishops, but only by obtaining the concurrence of the papacy.

---

1. Thomas J. Reese, *Inside the Vatican: The Politics and Organization of the Catholic Church* (Cambridge: Harvard University Press, 1996), 24.

In the Roman Church, the appointment and seating of bishops has been the sole prerogative of the pope only since the nineteenth century. He is aided in selection by a sizable bureaucracy that can find out—in a highly confidential process intended to prevent the selection from becoming a political brawl—a great deal about candidates for consecration. This process tends to select persons with unquestioned loyalty to the Holy See. Because their offices come initially from the papacy, bishops naturally give primary allegiance to the pope as a matter of loyalty and conviction as well as a matter of polity, but, once selected and consecrated, bishops hold office until they resign or die. In essence, their submission to the pope is insured by beliefs, customs, and commitments.

Preparation for Leadership

Ecclesiastical officials within a monarchical form of church governance are prepared for their roles through a long and structured assimilation into the institution over which they come to exercise their leadership. They are groomed (the theological term is *formed*) for such positions by years of training and experience. Monarchical episcopacy depends on a hierarchical process that insures that those eventually selected are thoroughly indoctrinated and conformed to the ethos of the church. Such persons have been tested within a structure that has definite expectations and within an apparatus that observes how well individuals conform to those expectations.

Many agencies have a hand in the training of such leaders and in the monitoring processes by which they are identified. In one regard, bishops are a bit like kings in stable political units. Kings in such political units are prepared for the leadership roles by long and faithful service within an institution with rules and conventions that preclude arbitrary decision making and unpredictable behavior. The difference, however, is that royalty usually comes to its positions by heredity, and everyone knows who is to be trained for the kingly or queenly role. Bishops emerge from a priesthood because of their leadership qualities; their identity is not determined by heredity. Even so, the institutional process tends to bring to the fore persons whose commitments have been thoroughly tested.

Officials of the Roman Catholic Church also include those with other titles, some honorary; others hold special yet limited powers. The title of *monsignor* is essentially honorary—often bestowed on faculty in seminaries or on priests in parishes of unique visibility. The title of *cardinal,* or prince of the church, is bestowed by the pope on priests or bishops noted for distinguished service to the church, often on bishops in charge of important dioceses, but sometimes on persons who have rendered distinctive service in other ways. The cardinals assist the pope. They do not constitute an intermediate level of authority between the pope and the bishops. They have automatic voice and vote in ecumenical councils and can perform papal functions in churches outside Rome. Their chief decision-making role may be, not so much to assist a living pope, but to carry on the governance of the church between the death of one pope and the election of another. They also serve as the electors of a new pope in a process in which they are sealed from the world to insure that their deliberations are not subject to manipulation by interest groups.

PRESERVERS OF TRADITION

Although bishops are predictably representative of an ongoing tradition, this does not mean that bishops are carbon copies of each other, or that there are no differences between them. The monarchical structure of the church does not eliminate personal variations among bishops. But such variations are usually about matters peripheral to the doctrinal orthodoxy and institutional orthopraxis which it is the bishop's duty to defend and advance. Monarchical bishops are not likely to be innovators or ecclesiastical upstarts. Their role is one of preserving rather than changing the customary patterns and fundamental convictions of the church. They exercise this preserving role both by teaching/ exemplifying and by administering/cajoling.

Moreover, monarchical bishops, like many earthly sovereigns, exercise their role with highly visible paraphernalia: special dress, attendants and aides, a building of which they are essentially the proprietors, and pageantry that gives their role uniqueness. Although many bishops are persons of extraordinary achievements—linguistic abilities, scholarly learning, administrative experience, and political acumen—their authority derives less from respect for such achievements than for their office. Members of churches with a monarchical polity are inculturated to respect the bishop, due not as much to personal charm or individual abilities as to the symbolic representation of the tradition vested in his role.

Much is made in the thinking of the Roman Catholic Church about "the historic episcopate" or "apostolic succession." The emphasis is on continuity with the tradition. While most discussion of these terms concerns (legitimately enough for sacramental theology) ordaining priests to preside at the Eucharist, which only a bishop can do, the concept of apostolic succession also has significance for governance. The idea of historic continuity is an important source of the aura that surrounds the office of bishop. The bishop is presumed to carry the apostolic mandate that derives from the Christ himself. However, "[bishops] are styled successors of the apostles, but not successors of Christ."[2] In Roman Catholic polity, this tradition includes legislative, judicial, and executive roles, but those roles are legitimized by the bishop's exemplification of the apostolic heritage initiated in New Testament times.

THE ROLE OF BISHOPS

One of the terms frequently used to describe a bishop helps catch the subtle yet crucial mix of authority and nurture combined in the office. Bishops are called "shepherds," and one of the symbols carried by the bishop is a shepherd's crook, or crosier. Shepherds have authority and lead their sheep in beneficial ways, but shepherds do not conduct rap sessions with their flocks to find the best grazing. The authority of shepherds derives from the care and nurture they provide for the flock rather than from the con-

---

2. Joseph Urtasun, *What Is a Bishop?* translated from the French by P. J. Hepburne-Scott (New York: Hawthorne Books, 1962), 40.

sent they obtain from below. The sheep depend on and benefit from the shepherd, whose care for the sheep is one of deep and compassionate obligation. It would be out of keeping for bishops to carry a whip or lash as a symbol of their role—though sometimes people think that individual bishops would be more honest if they did. Nor would it be appropriate to regard bishops as cowboys, one of whose skills is breaking in horses who have not yet been tamed. There is no place, even in monarchical episcopacy, for the symbolism of the lasso.

The expectations and duties of the Roman Catholic bishop are enormous. He is looked on to exemplify Christian fidelity in its most rigorous form. He is to seek perfection of his personal spirituality. He is expected to perform sacramental and ceremonial functions, not only the eucharistic celebration reserved for the priesthood, but also ceremonies like confirmation and ordination over which he presides; the bishop can deputize confirmations but not ordinations; he is to legislate, not only the rules and regulations that govern his own diocese but, in company with other bishops and in submission to the pope, policies directing the life of the larger church; he is expected to be a teacher, not so much by engaging himself in classroom pedagogy, but in seeing that the teaching of the church is properly done and that doctrine is rightly interpreted; he is an administrator, on whom rests the ultimate responsibility for the care of the diocesan property, finances, and personnel; he is an organizer, who builds and sustains community; and he is a pastor, who cares for the persons in his area of jurisdiction, especially the priests who depend on him for support and nurture. While the bishop does not do all these things by himself, he is responsible for seeing that others do them on his behalf and according to his judgment as to what the church requires.

Both the strength and fragility of Roman Catholic polity lie in this centralization of the leadership role in an able figure. This polity provides visibility and continuity to the institution over which episcopacy (both that of the bishops and that of the pope as chief bishop) presides. Although the polity does not necessarily eliminate diversity, it provides a clear way to keep diversity within manageable bounds. Everyone knows who adjudicates controversies and settles disputes. In theory, the doctrine of primacy of the pope precludes further agitation once an issue is settled at the highest level. But that intended consequence has not always been achieved as fully as often supposed.[3]

The weakness of Roman Catholic polity stems from the same source as its strength. The polity does not provide sufficient flexibility and lay involvement to deal with demands for change that will not die. Moreover, because no individual can do all that is expected of bishops, the responsibilities get delegated into bureaucracies that may not be easy to monitor and that resist change more naturally than they foster innovation. Such bureaucracies often imprison those who are their supposed directors.

The governance of the Roman Catholic Church is shaped by a body of canon law, which gives detailed directions for dealing with almost every imaginable problem. The church is served by a body of experts in canon law, many of whom have specialized doctorates that signify high proficiency in the interpretation and application of the church's legislation. Such proficiency does not come from taking one short course in polity in the seminary! Mastery of the intricacies of canon law is one of the ways in which the bureaucracy of the church maintains its position. Bishops do their work according to this law. The more than five hundred provisions of the canon law that direct their work are discussed in various manuals. The headings in one such manual provide a clue to the scope and nature of the bishop's duties. The headings are "The Bishop's Sanctifying Ministry"; "The Bishop's Teaching Ministry"; "The Bishop's Pastoral Government Ministry"; and "The Bishop in His Relationship to Various Members of the People of God."[4]

The section dealing with the bishop's sanctifying ministry covers duties that relate to a bishop's responsibility for insuring the liturgical validity of the sacraments performed within the diocese and the participation of the faithful in the obligations of the spiritual life. The sacraments include baptism; confirmation (done

---

3. The primacy of the pope has given rise to use of the term *infallibility,* but it is a formal characterization and less functional than often supposed. Papal infallibility has been invoked on only two occasions, which means it has not been the primary aspect of papal rule.

4. National Conference of Catholic Bishops, *A Manual for Bishops: Rights and Responsibilities of Diocesan Bishops in the Revised Code of Canon Law,* rev. ed. (Washington, D.C.: U.S. Catholic Conference, 1992).

only with the bishop's approval, but not necessarily by the bishop himself); the Eucharist; penance; anointing of the sick; ordination; and marriage. Performance of the sacraments is governed by numerous requirements concerning when, how, and by whom each is to be carried out. Many lay Catholics assume that the services of the church are properly conducted, and they do not concern themselves with mastering the details of canon law. Not a few, however, have come up against the provisions of canon law dealing with marriage—particularly when contemplating a marriage between persons of different faith traditions or when one or both of the parties have been divorced. The church attempts to uphold a well-defined conception of marriage. Priests frequently have to work closely with, and obtain the concurrence of, the bishop when dealing with marriages that do not fit normal expectations. These matters often become the locus of the episcopate's most immediate and least welcome interaction with the laity.

The rubric of sanctifying ministry also involves the bishops in the supervision of other worship activities—such as dedicating (or desacralizing) places of worship; supervising the cultic use of images and relics; and determining the observance of feast and penitential days. The bishop is also directly involved in decisions concerning the erection of church buildings.

The second major group of duties concerns the bishop as a teacher of the faith. The main obligation of the bishop is to insure that Catholic theology and practice are rightly understood. Bishops do this directly through their own preaching and indirectly by staying aware of the preaching done by priests. They see that catechetical instruction takes place for new converts. They establish and run parochial schools. They are responsible for seeing that those who teach (especially theology) are sound in doctrine. They examine (or have examined by trusted experts) the content of books and other publications written by Catholic authors that deal with matters of faith and practice and certify they contain nothing contrary to the faith. The teaching function of the bishops is exercised collegially from time to time through pastoral letters issued in company with other bishops from a given area, examining major issues confronting the church and society. Within the diocese, the bishop's teaching function is likely to be protective and conserving; in the pastoral letters issued by the bishops collectively, it is apt to be more challenging and illuminating and, on occasions, even controversial.

The governance role of bishops in pastoral matters is wide-ranging, detailed, and, subject to oversight by higher church authorities, authoritative. It is not necessarily carried out without the benefit of group process, but all groups that assist the bishop in the governance function must function through his authority. Episcopal councils, diocesan synods, and presbyterial and pastoral groups all assist the bishop but do not make policy apart from or above the bishop.

The bishop has the right of appointments, not only to a large number of special diocesan positions, but to the pastoral leadership of individual parishes under his care. Contrary to popular assumptions, pastoral appointments made by the bishop cannot be terminated without cause or ended suddenly—though the processes for determining whether these conditions apply are directed by the bishop, so it often appears that he can shift appointments at will. Canon law provides some protections for pastors, which, while by no means adding up to tenure, is more protection than that usually enjoyed by hourly workers in business and commerce.

The provisions of canon law that delegate to the bishop administrative control of temporalities vest in him the control of church-owned properties in his diocese. The bishop becomes an executive and financial officer, although more of a trust officer than a sole proprietor. He is responsible for both raising and distributing the church's sources of support. He is charged especially to provide sustenance to the clergy under his care, during both their active service and retirements. Bishops cannot dispose of church property at mere whim, but they must follow certain procedures.

Handling such resources is no small task since, in many dioceses, the church possesses much property, both in real estate and endowment funds. The typical diocese also raises money from contributions and sometimes from productive ventures it controls. The bishop's permission is needed in writing for many actions related to diocesan finances—if, for instance, an administrator feels that civil proceedings are necessary (either as plaintiff or defendant). The bishop must be involved when "pious wills" that designate the church as a beneficiary are drawn up or their proceeds distributed.

THE ROLE OF CANON LAW

Canon law specifies both the rights and the responsibilities of church members. The bishop is obligated to maintain the balance between protecting their rights and assuring that they meet their responsibilities. The bishop has authority over each category of the faithful, though naturally the exercise of such duties is felt more directly by clerics and members of religious orders than by the laity. The canon law governing the actions of bishops also specifies how bishops relate to persons and groups not in full communion with the church.

On the parish level, canon law makes two provisions. Canon 536 provides, subject to the judgment of the diocesan bishop, for the establishment of parish pastoral councils—composed of church members—to assist the priest in the pastoral activity of the parish. Canon 537 mandates the establishment of parish finance councils to assist the priest in the administration of parish goods. Committees may also be formed, under the authority of the parish councils, to deal with such matters as liturgy, continuing education, social mission, and so on. The role of pastoral and the finance councils (as well as that of any committee formed under them) is consultative. The pastor has the final say in the affairs of the parish.

Monarchical episcopacy is designed to provide governance in which there is a maximum of dependability and a minimum of haggling among groups with contesting agendas. It tends to produce continuity in policies and procedures, to emphasize the importance of law rather than spontaneity, and to give equal attention to liturgical/symbolic matters and to moral/logistical matters. It is apt to be more at home with the exercise of authority than carried away by the appeal of charisma. It provides avenues of service for the faithful and restricts service to carefully defined forms that respect and advance the tradition. It respects and rewards devoted fidelity. In this polity, it is possible to pursue an ecclesiastical career by making choices acceptable to the system. Dependence on popular whim and political approval for access to office or for attainment of goals is relatively low. It is probably a polity better suited to maintaining order than to overcoming chaos, to building empires than to meeting the needs of frontiers.

But, like any human organization, monarchical church government cannot escape the political element entirely. The bureaucracy that serves the church is not immune from the many devices by which persons wield influence and obtain decisions they favor, and for which they can obtain support by political maneuvering. Although the political element is usually covert in the bureaucracy, it is not absent. Sometimes the tensions are between different levels of the bureaucracy. The political process in bureaucracy works not according to open parliamentary procedures but through interaction among influential individuals who have access to each other and who can influence decisions by the top authorities.

EPISCOPAL CONFERENCES AND SYNODS

The political aspect of monarchical episcopacy becomes more apparent when the bishops work together for common objectives, namely in episcopal conferences (meetings of all the bishops whose diocese lies in a given nation) and in ecumenical councils (meetings of bishops from the entire world). Both of these gatherings operate as parliamentary bodies, although they are subject to papal review. Here debates over teaching and legislation are not unknown, and the witness of the bishops is not always univocal.

The 1983 Code of Canon Law mentions eighty-four matters that can be decided by episcopal conferences.[5] Many of these issues are minor; others are substantial. This gathering of bishops in the United States is called the National Conference of Catholic Bishops. It is an august body, staffed with able helpers, and it functions according to *Robert's Rules of Order*. Not only does it deal with matters of church discipline that can be addressed on this

---

5. For a helpful study of one episcopal conference, see Thomas J. Reese, S.J., *A Flock of Shepherds: The National Conference of Catholic Bishops* (Kansas City, Mo.: Sheed and Ward, 1992).

level, but it periodically issues pastoral letters that contain moral teaching about such momentous public issues as the economy, population policy (touching on both birth control and abortion), the church's attitude toward women, and nuclear war.

The Vatican reviews the work of such conferences and can rein in conclusions that venture too far from official teaching or policy. In drawing up major policy statements (called pastoral letters), the American bishops hold hearings that allow members of the church and even the public to provide information and viewpoints, but the bishops alone settle on the positions finally promulgated. Such social teaching does not—as it must under several church polities considered below—require the approval of a deliberative body composed of selected or elected representatives of the church, including laity.[6]

Following the Second Vatican Council, the idea of a synod of bishops was reinstituted. This is an international group of bishops, consisting of representatives from various regions, who serve in this capacity when called on by the pope. Such synods are of various types—ordinary, extraordinary, and special. They are advisory to the pope, and, unless he delegates legislative authority, they have no power in themselves. While these synods have to some degree helped increase the idea of collegiality, they have not fulfilled the hope of liberals within the church that the centralized power of the Roman Curia (or Vatican bureaucracy) would be more responsive to grassroots yearnings for change.

The highest level of collegiality within the Roman Catholic Church is the ecumenical council. Ecumenical councils once had a significant role in the church and determined both doctrine and governance. But with the centralization of authority in the papacy instigated by the Council of Trent, following the Reformation, the practice of holding ecumenical councils was all but eclipsed. The twentieth ecumenical council (Vatican I) was held in 1869–70. Interestingly, it strengthened the primacy of the papacy. In contrast, Vatican II (1962–66), the most recent ecumenical council, gave strong (albeit temporary) hope to those who favor greater collegiality in church governance.

---

6. Reese, *Inside the Vatican*, 33.

The frequency and duration of such councils varies. Many years can separate one council from another. Many councils meet for several sessions spread over months (even years). All bishops, cardinals, and the heads of religious orders attend. Much preparatory work is done to prepare for their deliberations, and the actions of the council come out as documents (decrees) that significantly influence the direction of the church for some time. Ecumenical councils in the contemporary church can meet and deliberate only at the behest and under the supervision of the pope. They are in no sense deliberative bodies with independent power to determine policy. Nevertheless, particularly when the papacy plays a supportive role, they can make significant changes. Councils can also host strong debate among groups with differing views.

Monarchical episcopacy depends on both custom and law and works best when accepted with fidelity and obedience. It emphasizes continuity and unity rather than change and diversity. It creates massive and effective organizational structures and is associated with impressive liturgical meaning and ritual symbolism. But it can be confounded by challenges too persistent to be thwarted from the top, and it tends to make participation of laity a matter of accepting ordained leaders' decisions.

RESOURCES FOR UNDERSTANDING ROMAN CATHOLICISM

Beal, John P., James A. Coriden, and Thomas J. Green, eds. *New Commentary on the Code of Canon Law.* Mahwah, N.J.: Paulist Press, 2000.

Dolan, John P. *Catholicism: An Historical Survey.* Woodbury, N.Y.: Barron's Educational Series, 1968.

Gillis, Chester. *Roman Catholicism in America.* New York: Columbia University Press, 1999.

Green, Thomas J. *A Manual for Bishops: Rights and Responsibilities of Diocesan Bishops in the Revised Code of Canon Law.* Rev. ed. Washington, D.C.: U.S. Catholic Conference, 1992.

Jiménez Urresti, Teodoro, ed. *Structures of the Church.* New York: Herder and Herder, 1970.

Küng, Hans. *Structures of the Church.* Translated from the German by Salvator Attanasio. New York: Thomas Nelson and Sons, 1964.

Reese, Thomas J. *A Flock of Shepherds: The National Conference of Catholic Bishops*. Kansas City, Mo.: Sheed and Ward, 1992.

————. *Inside the Vatican: The Politics and Organization of the Catholic Church*. Cambridge, Mass. and London: Harvard University Press, 2000.

Swidler, Leonard, and Arlene Swidler, eds. *Bishops and People*. Philadelphia: Westminster Press, 1970.

2

Managerial Episcopacy

A LTHOUGH THE GOVERNANCE of Methodist churches is similar to that of Catholic churches in the extent to which ecclesiastical life is tightly controlled, the life of the two churches is different and the ethos of the two groups hardly comparable. While both function through bishops and bishops' power, explaining the contrast between their polities requires different terminology. In Catholicism, for reasons explored in the last chapter, the appropriate terminology is *monarchical episcopacy*; in Methodism, for reasons suggested here, the term is *managerial episcopacy*.

Methodist Governance

The life and operation of the United Methodist Church, the largest group of Methodists in the United States, is governed by a book of several hundred pages entitled *The Book of Discipline*. This book is updated every four years and has grown over more than two hundred years. Over time, experience has prompted legislative actions that have refined ways of dealing with old circumstances and provided ways to meet new challenges. Although much of this book, like a good deal of Catholic canon law, specifies procedures for governance, other equally important parts deal with the church's history, its doctrinal standards, its duties to society, and the establishment of agencies through which the church seeks to carry on both its own affairs and its witness to the wider world. Complete mastery of its contents would require a major professional investment, but living under its provisions is possible because the governance works with carefully structured regularity (one might say "methodically").

A Methodist bishop has as much control over the placement and function of clergy as does a Roman Catholic bishop, but the source of authority is different, and the ethos that surrounds the office varies considerably. Indeed, Methodist governance is different in many respects from all other traditions that govern by bishops. It employs a different vocabulary for describing many of the same aspects of governance found in other forms of episcopacy—a vocabulary which indicates the operational differences between Methodism and other churches, even other churches with episcopal governance. Understanding Methodism involves learning its special vocabulary.

When Methodism first established the office of bishop in the United States the term *superintendent* was used. The section of *The Book of Discipline* that deals with the role and functions of the episcopacy still carries the title "The Superintendency." We probably should, if the sound of the language encouraged it, speak of "superintendency episcopacy," but "managerial episcopacy" conveys practically the same concept and is easier to articulate. Moreover, the phrase "management of ministry" is used with some frequency and has significance in describing the Methodist approach to ecclesiastical governance. Managerial episcopacy is concerned primarily with making the church function effectively. It views the office of bishop in functional terms, as involving managerial skills, rather than giving it theological dimensions or sacerdotal significance.[1] The *Book of Discipline* describes the role and function of the bishop in the following way:

> The task of superintending in the United Methodist Church resides in the office of bishop and extends to the district superintendent, with each possessing distinct and collegial responsibilities. The mission of the Church is to make disciples of Jesus Christ.... From apostolic times, certain ordained persons have been entrusted with the particular tasks of superintending. The purpose of superintending is to equip the Church in its

---

1. One book of essays that deals with patterns of episcopacy in other traditions does not include Methodists. This suggests that the Methodist superintendency is not regarded by many as being in the same mode of ecclesiastical governance as churches with historic episcopacies. See Peter Moore, ed., *Bishops, but What Kind? Reflections on Episcopacy* (London: SPCK, 1982).

disciple-making ministry. Those who superintend carry primary responsibility for ordering the life of the church. It is their task to enable the gathered Church to worship and evangelize faithfully.

It is also their task to facilitate the initiation of structures and strategies for the equipping of Christian people for service in the Church and in the world in the name of Jesus Christ and to help extend the service in mission. It is their task, as well, to see that all matters, temporal and spiritual, are administered in a manner that acknowledges the ways and insights of the world critically and with understanding while remaining cognizant of and faithful to the mandate of the Church.[2]

The Development of Methodist Governance

The governance of the Methodist Church, particularly in the United States, has from the beginning emerged more from efforts to meet the needs of society than from efforts to continue a historic set of practices. This does not mean that the Methodist Church has thrown scripture or church history onto the junk pile, but both in the original formation of its governance and in subsequent modifications, scripture and tradition have been applied in conjunction with reason and experience to respond to ongoing needs. Instead of stressing continuity in doctrine or in practice, the Methodist approach has made for governance that has changed as events have called on the church to do things in new ways. Moreover, Methodism stresses the doing of theology rather than inculcating conformity to creedal formulations.

An illustration of this process is found in the steady change in the place bishops have occupied in relationship to the church. When the office of bishop was first created in the American church, those elected constituted a group of leaders for the entire church. Even though the church convened in conferences by regions, at least several of the bishops were expected to attend regional gatherings as representatives of the whole denomination. They were to move around (itinerate) the whole church corporately, not simply to administer a single region assigned to them.

---

2. *The Book of Discipline of the United Methodist Church,* 1996, par. 401.

In theory, bishops are administrative and executive heads of the church.[3]

As the country grew and as the church enlarged, this moving around became less practical. Particular bishops became associated with particular regions. Today, as has been true since the early part of the twentieth century, individual bishops are associated with particular annual (regional) conferences. Although this makes it seem that bishops' relationship to the churches in the area they govern is like that of lifetime diocesan bishops in other versions of episcopacy, the structure and exercise of their role is significantly different. Because they preside over a conference only for a given term, Methodist bishops may be said to have a tenuous rather than a tenured relationship to their conferences.

Methodism is a highly connectional system marked by a high degree of control. This gives it a capacity to minister to areas of need, to engage in mission efforts to reach places that have not yet developed stable parish life, and to be assured that the ministries of churches within the system conform to the denomination's expectations. This stance goes back to the Wesleys themselves, who were adamant that the movement they founded would be supervised to achieve maximum effectiveness and to guarantee procedural regularity. This made Methodism effective on the American frontier; it did not have to wait for people to establish themselves and then to call their ministers. The ministers moved westward with the people, sometimes ahead of them.

Methodism trusts authority and uses authority to advance the cause of the gospel. Its governance pattern developed in an era in which efficiency was becoming a desired goal in the culture as a whole, when the business world was developing complex logistical systems, and when decisions, more than heritage, were seen as influential in human affairs. These cultural developments undoubtedly influenced the way the church thought about its business. Ecclesiastical affairs would be marked by the same logistical rigor as commercial ventures.

The spirituality associated with Methodism is characterized by

---

3. James K. Mathews, *Set Apart to Serve: The Meaning and Role of Episcopacy in the Wesleyan Tradition* (Nashville: Abingdon Press, 1985), chap. 5.

devotion to service. The pattern of governance utilizes ministers by assigning them where their talents are most needed. Acceptance of ordination at the senior level carries willingness to serve when and where directed. This has come to be true even of the bishops themselves. They are subject to reassignment among annual conferences even as the clergy are subject to reassignment from parish to parish within the conference to which they belong. The only difference is that bishops can only be reassigned every four or eight years (in rare cases, twelve years), although the clergy can be reassigned more frequently. This system, know as *itinerancy,* is the most distinguishing feature of Methodism. Leadership positions within the system do not depend on lifetime associations built on the cultivation of long-standing spheres of local influence. It is frequently said, as a means of comparing this view of ministry with that of other denominations, that in many polities ministers are "called," but in Methodist polity they are "sent." This affects in important ways how it feels to arrive in a new pastorate. It also has a subtle but nevertheless discernible influence on the way in which ministers and congregations relate to each other.

There have been times in Methodist history when this system has required a high degree of trusting subordination. Assignments to *charges*—the term for a pastorate or other ministerial position— were often made without consultation. Ministers could attend their annual conference without knowing where they would be assigned the next year; they might have to be in a new location the next Sunday. At one time the system of itinerancy involved frequent and regular moves, with short tenures in any one place (or charge), but this pattern also has been changing. Ministers and congregations generally knew, however, when the time for changing pastorates had come. Sudden, unscheduled changes, like those that occur under a monarchical system, do not take place except in unforeseeable crisis.

Over the years, the process of appointment has become more consultative in practice. Longer stays in one place are becoming more common where a pastorate is going well. Ministers in important churches—in the "top" locations—have always stayed longer than those in ordinary charges. Ministers of the conference assigned to nonparochial duties—such as teachers in colleges or seminaries—have generally remained in these assignments for long periods.

One consequence of this system is that local congregations are generally receptive to whatever minister is sent. This does tend to give ministry an objective quality that is not dependent on the personal characteristics of individuals or the quirky expectations of parishes. This system also has several consequences that can reinforce the effectiveness of ministry. It tends to guarantee greater freedom of the pulpit; the minister is not a local congregation's hired hand and cannot be dismissed by local action. The appointment system avoids the protracted interims that churches that call their ministers undergo when changing pastors. It allows for the most effective deployment of talents within the conference. One of the most valuable consequences of this polity, possibly unintended when it was created, has been the relative success Methodists have had in placing women and minorities in parish situations. Such openings would not have occurred in a system in which congregations look for congenial leadership reflecting their own predispositions.[4]

Because of itinerancy there are no Methodist cathedrals. Since the role of the bishop in liturgy is far less prominent in Methodism than in most episcopally governed churches, the bishop can function without a designated sanctuary. However, bishops are provided with central offices and with living quarters from which they can travel within the conference and to the many meetings that fulfill their connectional responsibilities. These living quarters are not necessarily located near a church building or adjacent to the bishop's office.

Methodist bishops do not consistently wear distinctive attire. Since they are sacramentally and liturgically of the same order as ministers in full connection with the conference, their vestments are likely to be similar to those of parish clergy. Since Methodism was actively involved in serving the American frontier, it often dispensed with vestments for the sake of convenience. The practice of both bishops and elders (ordained ministers) on these matters today is largely a matter of individual choice, rather than an

---

4. Some of these points are taken from ibid., 203f.

identifiable pattern that contributes significantly to creating a distinctive ethos (unless unpredictable variation can be considered an ethos).

CONFERENCES

Methodism determines church policy in conferences, which function as deliberative bodies. There are several levels of such conferences, each with its own duties and powers. The basic corporate body is the annual conference, which consists of clergy and lay delegates in equal numbers from all churches in a given geographical area (usually a small state or portion of a large state), together with the officers of Methodist organizations from the same area and youth delegates. The annual conference provides the locus of clergy membership and also elects delegates to other conferences. Its primary function is to connect local churches to one another. In a number of conference actions, the clergy members vote separately from the lay delegates, particularly on matters relating to the trial and admission of persons to membership (conference membership of some sort being necessary to clergy status), and in the election of ministerial delegates to other conferences. The laity, in turn, separately elect the lay delegates to the same conferences. All ordinations take place at the annual conference and not, as in many polities, at a church associated with the life or ministry of the ordinand, or at a cathedral. The location of the ordinations signifies the centrality of the annual conference as the locus of ministerial identity. There are two orders of clergy in Methodist polity: that of *elders*, who itinerate; and that of permanent *deacons*, who stay in their home parishes as assistants.[5]

The highest deliberative body in Methodism is the *General Conference*. This meets in April or May of every fourth year and legislates general policy for the church as a whole. It is composed of delegates elected by the annual conferences—half clergy delegates elected by the ministers, and half lay delegates elected by

5. Previously, the diaconate was a step on the way to becoming an elder rather than a permanent order of ministry. This previous system also included an order of diaconal ministers, who served in many of the same ways as the current order of permanent deacons.

the laity.[6] The powers of the General Conference give it broad authority to direct the life of the church.

The annual conferences are grouped geographically into *jurisdictional conferences*, of which there are presently five in the United States. Much of the church's program is carried on by these jurisdictional conferences, which can define the boundaries of the annual conferences. Jurisdictional conferences also elect bishops, who serve at least four years in the conference that elected them but who then can be assigned through the College of Bishops to work in a different area. Each jurisdictional conference has its own College of Bishops, which meets three or four times a year to deal with regional matters.

Methodist polity also provides for other conferences. *Central conferences* are concerned with the work of the church outside the United States. Churches within a specific area of an annual conference may assemble in *district conferences*. Finally, annual meetings among local congregations or groups of contingent congregations, to which a member of an annual conference is assigned, are known as *charge conferences*.

BISHOPS AND DISTRICT SUPERINTENDENTS

Methodism is firmly attached to the importance of episcopacy, but it utilizes the institution on its own terms. The constitution of the church contains several restrictive rules. One of the most basic is rule number 3, which, although disarmingly simple in its wording, is loaded with significant implications. Referring to the legislative powers of the denomination's highest governing body, this rule says, "The General Conference shall not change or alter any part or rule of our governance, so as to do away with episcopacy or destroy the plan of our itinerant general superintendency."[7]

Bishop James K. Mathews, in his study of Methodist episcopacy, has pointed out how several key words in this brief provision have crucial implications. Inserting explanatory parentheses, he elabo-

---

6. The Constitution of the United Methodist Church as contained in Part I of *The Book of Discipline*, div. 2, sec. VI, art. IV and art. V (par. 33 and 34 in *The Book of Discipline*, 1996).

7. Ibid., div. 2, sec. III, art. III (par. 17).

rates the provision as follows: "The General Conference (by simple legislative action) shall not change or alter any rule of our government so as to *do away* with episcopacy or destroy the *plan* of (not dogma or assumption such as divine right) *our* (our own peculiar history and understanding, experience, custom, usage, and model relating to the episcopal office; as opposed, say, to a view such as apostolic succession) *itinerant* (not merely limited, localized, or diocesan) *general* (churchwide) *superintendency* (executive supervision)."[8]

The executive function of the bishop includes a number of powers—particularly those associated with the appointment of clergy to charges—but these powers are attended by limitations on the bishop's role in policy making. When bishops are elected, they cease to be voting members of the annual conferences with which they have been associated. They can preside but they cannot vote, even though their ministerial status is the same as that of elders (ordained ministers in full connection with the conference). Nor do the bishops act collegially to make fundamental policy for the church—a function vested in the legislative powers of the General Conference. There is an analogy here to the separation of powers between legislative and executive branches of the U.S. government. Bishops execute the policies made by a legislative body composed of both clergy and laity, but they do not make those policies directly. The analogy to the U.S. government is further evident in the provision for a judicial council, which handles constitutional cases and other matters, including appeals from the decisions of bishops.[9]

All bishops, including those who have retired, belong to a collegiate body called the Council of Bishops. They are members by virtue of their office as bishop, but they do not derive standing from this council. Their membership cannot be bestowed or terminated by their peers. The Council of Bishops is an instrument for making the church's general superintendency a matter of joint concern. The council cannot legislate new policy nor can it exercise judicial functions, but bishops can arrive at strategies to help

---

8. Mathews, *Set Apart to Serve*, 199f.
9. See division 4 of the Methodist Constitution.

them to carry out the executive function more adequately and more consistently for the benefit of the church. This is done collegially. No individual occupies, either by election or appointment, an office as "head" of the entire church.

Bishops report that their membership in the Council of Bishops is a source of encouragement and peer support for themselves and their families.[10] One of the burdens of itinerancy is the difficulty of developing local associations and friendships that reinforce a person in ministry. A gathering of peers that does not have to make policy or pass judicial judgments can help overcome the quasi-isolation that comes, not only from itinerancy, but from holding an office that commands respect yet that deters many from sharing intimacies. It may offer a place to let down one's guard.

Clergy in particular are apt to put their best face forward as they deal with their bishop and, in turn, the bishop is likely to behave similarly. Such behavior is not necessary in a group of peers, where they cannot exercise power over each other. Although the bishops have peer support in their council, the ministers who have local charges, even though in theory the annual conference is supposed to fulfill this function, do not always enjoy a helpful level of collegial support. At the annual conferences, higher officials are always watching.

Methodist bishops are expected to do many things. Their leadership is considered both spiritual and temporal, and they are authorized by *The Book of Discipline* to "guard the faith, order, liturgy, doctrine, and discipline of the Church; to seek and be a sign of the unity of the faith; to exercise the discipline of the whole Church; to supervise and support the Church's life, work, and mission throughout the world; and to lead all persons entrusted to their oversight in worship, in the celebration of the sacraments, and in their mission of witness and service to the world."[11]

Other provisions in *The Book of Discipline* spell out this general mandate in more specific terms. Many provisions cite the presidential (presiding) duties of bishops; their role in ordaining elders and deacons; their responsibilities in the appointment process;

---

10. Mathews, *Set Apart to Serve*, 226f. Undoubtedly matters arise over which bishops disagree, so such meetings do not avoid political tensions entirely.

11. *Book of Discipline*, 1996, par. 404.

and their duty to see that the polity of the church is carried out constructively. *The Book of Discipline* emphasizes the legitimacy of cooperation with other churches. Methodism has never had doctrinal reservations about participating in ecumenical relationships, even though its governance is in many ways unique and not easily meshed with the polities of other bodies.

Bishops do not bear their responsibilities individually. One of the unique features of Methodist governance is a structure of official leadership through which the supervisory function takes place. The bishops work through district superintendents. These are members of the clergy appointed by a bishop to maintain direct contact with all the churches and ministers in a given area (called a district) of the annual conference. They act as liaisons between the local parishes and the bishop. These positions are usually filled by ordained ministers of some experience and maturity who can inspire and cajole churches and clergy toward a spiritually and temporally fruitful stewardship. The several district superintendents in a conference are called the bishop's cabinet.[12] The district superintendent presides at the charge conferences. While the charge conference includes local leadership and meets at the local church, it is not the equivalent of a congregational meeting but is an instrument through which the episcopacy exercises its superintending role. These meetings serve an important function, not only in inspiring effective ministry but in providing information that helps in the appointment process. A good district superintendent (or "DS") also uses the charge conference to cultivate the leadership of the laity.

The Book of Discipline of 1996 contains instructive language about the nature and functions of the superintendents. The language applies to both bishops and the district superintendents who are members of their cabinets. The language helps reveal the Methodist understanding of leadership and offers a significant clue to the ethos that superintendency creates within the denomination:

---

12. The bishop and the district superintendents constitute the appointments cabinet. In many conferences, staff persons may be added to deal with other affairs, in which case the cabinet is called a program cabinet.

Guidelines for Superintending in This Age: The demands of this age on the leadership of bishops and district superintendents in the United Methodist Church can be seen in mode, pace, and skill.

1. *Mode*—Leaders need to be able to read consensus and integrate it into a living tradition, to be open to the prophetic word, to be skilled in team-building, and to be effective in negotiation. The style of leadership should rise out of nurtured and cultivated spiritual disciplines and patterns of holiness, for the Spirit is given to the community and its members to the extent they participate.

2. *Pace*—Beyond formal systems of accountability, leaders need to open themselves to forms of accountability that they cultivate for themselves through a support group. Such a group can listen, can help and can clarify, as well as participate with the leader, as he or she thinks through time demands and constraints in the process of sorting out priorities. Appropriate time must be taken for reflection, developing friendships and self-renewal.

3. *Skill*—Among the skills needed by leaders are spiritual discipline, theological reflection, building the unique community of the church and of the larger community as well. Reading the signs of the times, analyzing, designing strategy, assessing needs, organizing a wide range of resources, and evaluating programs and personnel are yet other skills crucial for leaders.[13]

Bishops are considered to have educational responsibilities. Some Methodist bishops have been chosen from among academics, and some are scholars of merit. They can educate by what they say in church meetings, by the preaching they do as they travel, and, for some, by the books they write. However, they do not sponsor the creation of parochial schools or directly supervise institutions of higher learning except (as would be true of laypersons) when they are members of such institutions' governing boards. Theological reflection and research in the United Methodist Church (as in much of Protestantism) is carried out with little or no support or interference from the episcopacy, and

---

13. *Book of Discipline*, 1996, par. 402.

may be stronger because of it. Nor do Methodist bishops oversee theological publications, as do Roman Catholic bishops.

Although it does not happen as regularly in the Methodist Church as in the Roman Catholic Church, the bishops do work jointly to carry on a teaching function. One of the most notable examples was the release in 1986 of the letter on nuclear warfare, *In Defense of Creation*. This was written in a similar process to that which the Roman Catholic bishops used in preparing their letter on the morality of nuclear weaponry. It is an equally thoughtful and impressive document, though neither was received without controversy in its respective church.

THE ROLE OF THE LAITY

We have already noted that Methodism undergoes small but significant transformations as it responds to changing circumstances in its ministry fields. Perhaps one of the most important of these transformations has been the way in which the laity have been incorporated into the workings of the church. Methodism sprang from English Anglicanism at a time when ordained priests were accustomed to exercising clerical initiatives. But Methodism's encounter with America required a dependence on local preachers with lay status, who served churches between the visits of ordained ministers. Methodism also developed an office of lay leader, a person associated with a local parish even as the appointed clergy came and went.

It is not possible to involve laity in these and other important roles without creating pressure to let them have a more significant place in governance. Resistance to the autocratic rule of bishops had become strong by the early nineteenth century. The issue was so keenly felt and hotly debated that a new group formed, the Methodist Protestant Church, which accepted Methodist doctrine but not episcopal governance. Methodism also split over slavery, but this did not involve disputes regarding governance. Methodist Episcopal Churches, North and South, continued to use the office of bishop in similar ways, yet also to develop increasingly important roles for lay leadership. Lay delegates were accepted in the General Conference by 1870 in the South and by 1872 in the North, and lay involvement in the deliberative and legislative bodies of the church has been important ever since.

Governance in contemporary Methodism is a shared responsibility of clergy and laity. Local churches have a church council composed of laypersons that makes many decisions on the parish level. Conference meetings seat lay and clergy delegates in equal numbers. Lay preachers and lay leaders continue to work in local parishes and to provide leadership that supplements that of the appointed elder. Although the ordained elders do have sacramental functions that are distinct from those of laity, the sacramental function is not the primary means by which clergy are usually identified. There is little sacramental clericalism in the Methodist ethos.

The focus of Methodist piety and spirituality has been on the cultivation of holiness. This involves prayer and Bible study but also exemplary behavior and moral rectitude. The expected holiness is compatible with living in the world, and laity as well as clergy can achieve it. For years, the use of alcohol and smoking have been frowned upon. Laity have been admonished to avoid alcohol and tobacco, and clergy have been required to do so (but insiders know there is some "winking" at the requirement). Although such discipline placed more pressure on the clergy to follow rules of wholesome deportment, they were not required to maintain a lifestyle appropriate only for a special group. This did not, however, prevent the application of a double standard in popular expectations—a situation by no means unique to Methodism.

BOARDS, AGENCIES, AND PROPERTY

Another feature of Methodism is the boards and agencies that carry on agendas that are national or international in scope. Provision for their establishment as well as the outline of their duties and responsibilities are spelled out in *The Book of Discipline*. This makes the boards constitutionally ordered and not merely administratively devised.

Properties in the United Methodist Church are owned in trust; that is, the title belongs to the local church or corresponding agency that possesses the property, but the use must meet the purposes of the whole church. The administration and care of each property is vested in a local board of trustees. Trustees are admonished in *The Book of Discipline* to administer all property in light of the social principles of the church.

Methodist governance, which has many unique features and its own vocabulary for delineating them, provides logistical agility in meeting the demands of the denomination, in holding the local churches in close connection, in dealing robustly with the surrounding society, and in utilizing theology as a tool for strengthening and illuminating the gospel under changing circumstances. It seeks to use scripture, tradition, reason, and experience (the Methodist quadrilateral) to enable the church to live its faith rather than to protect a given body of belief or practice. This polity does not preserve Methodism from internal differences (sometimes disagreements and even divisions), but it does offer a carefully defined and closely coordinated connectionalism that holds together remarkably well in spite of those differences.

Resources for Understanding Methodism

The Book of Discipline of the United Methodist Church. Nashville: United Methodist Publishing House, 1996, 2000.

Frank, Thomas Edward. *Polity, Practice, and the Mission of the United Methodist Church.* Nashville: Abingdon Press, 1997.

Kirby, James E. *The Episcopacy in American Methodism.* Nashville: Kingswood Books, 2000.

Kirby, James E., Russell E. Richey, and Kenneth E. Rowe. *The Methodists.* Westport, Conn.: Greenwood Press, 1996; Praeger, 1998.

Mathews, James K. *Set Apart to Serve: The Meaning and Role of Episcopacy in the Wesleyan Tradition.* Nashville: Abingdon Press, 1985.

Tuell, Jack M. *The Organization of the United Methodist Church.* Nashville: Abingdon Press, 1982.

Willimon, William H. *Why I Am a United Methodist.* Nashville: Abingdon Press, 1990.

3

Pastoral and Exemplary
Episcopacy

THE GOVERNANCE PATTERN described in this chapter, one version found in the Episcopal Church and the second in various branches of Orthodoxy, effectively embodies the ceremonial and symbolic functions of the bishop's role but accords the bishop only a limited amount of power to govern individual parishes.

EPISCOPAL GOVERNANCE

Those familiar with monarchical and managerial episcopacy are frequently surprised to learn that bishops in the Episcopal Church have to rely a great deal on persuasion to govern their dioceses. Although deference toward the bishop is often very high, and overt defiance of the bishop by priests and parishes is relatively rare, disagreements can take place within the Episcopal Church to a degree unimaginable under other forms of episcopacy. Moreover, the Episcopal Church often preserves its togetherness by allowing individual bishops and parishes to act, regarding many matters, on their own convictions, rather than by imposing strict demands for conformity. The Episcopal Church is better thought of as cohered around an ethos than as centrally controlled.

The worldwide Anglican communion is held together more by common experience of worship than by subscription to specific understandings of doctrine or by conformity to unique moral expectations. The most meaningful symbol of unity is a book of common prayer for worship. A great deal of biblical material and several historic creeds are embodied in these prayer books, but there is considerable variation in how the Bible and the creeds are understood. Many Episcopalians view this tolerance of dif-

ference as a source of their church's appeal and strength. As
W. Norman Pittenger has remarked, "Those of us who are of the
Episcopal Church think this is all to the good. We do not regret
the differences; we rejoice in them."[1]

Another symbol of unity is acceptance of the historic episcopacy. Belief in the historical episcopacy concerns the ordering of
the ministry within, and the apostolicity and catholicity of, the
church. Ordinations can only be conducted by bishops, who also
practice the "hands-on" confirmation of new church members.
These functions make the role of the bishop highly important and
very visible—but such activities are essentially liturgical rather
than managerial.

The Episcopal Church, particularly in the United States, is
modeled more on a representative democracy than on a monar-
chy. The bishop's role is more like that of a mentor who persuades
people to respect the policies and procedures of the church than
like an official who commands obedience. Authority in the church
combines broad representation expressed with a division of powers
between laity and clergy, between congregation and dioceses, and
between dioceses and the national church. This makes the governance of the church more complex and difficult to comprehend
than polities that draw clearly designated lines of authority and
that impose decisions on subordinate groups. It means that there
can be considerable difference among individual bishops as to
how they understand Christian faith and think about moral issues. While Episcopal bishops exhibit a great deal of conformity
in liturgy and similarity in their special vestments, they can vary
enormously in their theological positions, church practice, and
social advocacy.

I once heard it said of an Episcopal priest that "he is a man of
the book." The reference was not to the Bible, but to the *Book
of Common Prayer* (and at the time to the 1928 version of the
prayer book replaced by a 1967 revision). Tendencies to rigor and
perhaps even intransigence in the Episcopal Church generally express themselves, not as biblical literalism or rigorous moralism,

---

1. W. Norman Pittenger, *The Episcopalian Way of Life* (Englewood Cliffs, N.J.: Prentice-
Hall, 1957), 13.

but as strict observance of the liturgy of the prayer book utilized in a Catholic manner. The stance of a priest is frequently revealed in such seemingly incidental manners as how the priest performs the ablutions (that is, the ritual cleaning of hands, chalice, and paten used in the Eucharist). Meticulous care generally indicates a high-church stance, less fastidiousness more of a low-church orientation.

The governance structure of the Episcopal Church is set forth in the *Constitution and Canons for the Government of the Protestant Episcopal Church in the United States of America*. This is a book of fine print, roughly two hundred pages in length—the first nine pages of which contain the constitution and the remaining 190 the canons (roughly speaking, the bylaws). Both the first article in the constitution and the first item in the canons concern the General Convention, a bicameral body consisting of a House of Bishops and a House of Deputies. This governing body must meet at least once every three years, which means that matters of governance are not likely to be altered quickly.

Membership in the House of Bishops is automatic for bishops (all have voice, but retired bishops can no longer vote). Since many dioceses have more than one bishop, and since some bishops serve in nonparochial offices that they have assumed after election by a diocese, the membership of the House of Bishops is somewhat larger than the number of dioceses. The House of Deputies is composed of representatives chosen from each of the dioceses, consisting of equal numbers of priests (called *presbyters* in Episcopal polity, to distinguish them from deacons) and laity. The constitution provides for four priests and four lay delegates from each diocese, though this can be reduced to as few as two by the General Convention. Although both houses sit at the same time, each meets separately, and either group can initiate legislation. In order for legislation to be enacted it must have a majority vote of each house (concurrent majorities).

It is no accident that provisions for the General Convention are set forth first in the constitution. The ultimate authority for dealing with the church as a whole is vested in the General Convention, not in the episcopacy by itself. The government of the United States, with a Senate, House of Representatives, and an

executive branch, is frequently cited as an analogy, but the corre-
spondence is only approximate.[2] The subtle interplay of authority
and influence that marks this system has been described as follows:

> The principle of "checks and balances" also operates in the func-
> tioning of the episcopacy. A careful reading of the Constitution
> and Canons of the Episcopal Church and of most of its constituent
> dioceses will reveal that the bishop, for example, is able to do very
> few things on his own sole authority. Again and again he is obliged
> to secure the consent of this or that committee or group of advi-
> sors before his action can be taken as authoritative. No man can
> be ordained, for example, without a long series of approvals and
> recommendations in which the laity of the Church by their des-
> ignated representatives must participate. Although the bishop is
> given the authority of extending the work of the Church within
> the boundaries of his own diocese, the clergy and laity control the
> budgetary and financial support of such work, and therefore par-
> ticipate in the development of policy and program. The laity of the
> Episcopal Church may exercise the power of veto in all changes
> in the liturgy, in the election of bishops and on many other cen-
> trally important matters in church life. Obviously, the Episcopal
> Church, reflecting the spirit and ideals of the American Consti-
> tution, is thoroughly democratic and representative in its life and
> government.[3]

The Duties of Bishops

The *Constitution and Canons* contains many references to the duties and the obligations of bishops, but very little is mentioned
concerning their powers. They can perform ceremonial and liturgical actions reserved for their office (mainly confirmations of new
members, the ordinations of clergy, and the co-consecration of
other bishops), but these can be carried out only after many decisions by both clergy and laypersons. Most actions by the bishop
are taken only after consultation with a standing committee of

---

2. The House of Representatives and the Senate do act by concurrent majorities, but
the executive role of the president involves far more decision-making authority than is the
case with the bishops.

3. John McGill Krumm, *Why I Am an Episcopalian* (New York: Thomas Nelson and
Sons, 1957), 102f.

clerical and lay members elected (or selected) from the diocese. The wording of the canon that legitimizes standing committees suggests a combination of consultative and oversight roles.

> In every Diocese the Standing Committee shall elect from their own body a President and a Secretary. They may meet in conformity with their own rule from time to time, and shall keep a record of their proceedings; and they may be summoned to a special meeting wherever the President may deem it necessary. They may be summoned on the requisition of the Bishop, whenever the bishop shall desire their advice; and they may meet of their own accord and agreeably to their own rules when they may be disposed to advise the Bishop.[4]

The ability of the standing committee to take initiatives in governance is important for understanding Episcopal polity. As a matter of practice, the standing committee defers to the bishop in most matters, but has the power to offer advice and counsel. A pastoral bishop makes almost all decisions consultatively and collegially with representatives of the church.

In confirmations, the bishop is presented with persons who have been catechized and prepared by the rector (or priest in charge) of a local congregation and reviewed by the vestry. In ordinations, the bishop ordains only after extensive review of the candidates (postulants) has taken place. The review is conducted by a special commission on ministry designated for this purpose, which includes both clergy and laity from the diocese, but also by the diocesan standing committee. Candidates must complete seminary training (or its equivalent) and pass written general ordination examinations (or "GOEs") that are nationally administered.

Once a person is approved for ordination, it takes place in two steps. The first step, ordination to the diaconate, usually (but not always) occurs at the cathedral, because deacons in theory are directly responsible to the bishop and are assigned to work according to the bishop's judgment. In addition to the diaconate as a first step to the priesthood, a permanent diaconate is possible

---

4. *Constitution and Canons for the Government of the Protestant Episcopal Church in the United States of America*, 1997, title I, canon 12, sec. 1.

that is generally sought by persons who wish to represent the church in its ministry/service to the world and to interpret the needs, hopes, and concerns of the world to the church.

The second level of ordination, which occurs no sooner than six months after ordination to the diaconate, is to the priesthood. This step confers the power to be the celebrant at the Eucharist and to perform other sacramental actions (such as reconciliation, healing, marriage); it is a prerequisite to becoming rector of a church or to being a clergy member of the House of Delegates at the General Convention. This ordination often takes place in a church with which the person being ordained has some personal connection. It may be candidate's home church or the church in which the candidate will be a minister.

The bishop is also involved in dealing with resignations from the priesthood (or from the diaconate) but acts only with the advice and consent of the standing committee. The bishop oversees judicial processes for dealing with misconduct but does not have the power to impose punishments and sanctions apart from the consultative procedures required by the canons.

The ministers of the church are required to remain in contact with the bishop of the diocese in which they maintain ecclesiastical standing, and to report at least annually on their activities. When in charge of parishes as rectors, the clergy have a great deal of liberty to direct activities according to the good of the parish. An older wording is instructive: "The control of the worship and the spiritual jurisdiction of the Parish are vested in the Rector, subject to the Rubrics of the Book of Common Prayer, the Canons of the Church, and the godly counsel of the Bishop."[5] "Godly counsel" is symbolically important and, as a matter of procedural reality, functions with significance, but it does not denote controlling power.

Rectors direct the worship in their parish under the rubrics of the church, but they are not required to obtain the agreement of a parish committee of laypersons. Consultation is voluntary and may be important in keeping the parish appreciative, but it is

---

5. This wording is taken from the *Constitution and Canons*, 1979 (title III, canon 21, sec. 1[a]). By 1997, the wording had been changed to substitute the words "pastoral direction" for "godly counsel" (title III, canon 14, sec. 1[a]).

not mandatory. (Clergy in many other polities—especially those described in the following chapters—are constitutionally much more restricted by the wishes of the congregation concerning how services are conducted.)

CONSULTATIVE PROCESSES

Many canons of the church are devoted to the conditions that guide the selection, ordination, and obligations of those in the clerical role. But the canonical requirements, although carefully drawn and specific with respect to many matters, merely set up procedures that have input in discerning who is fit to become a minister. Few churches make the route to ordination slower or a process that involves more interaction between the candidates and the commission of clergy and laity than the Episcopal Church. As a former seminary professor who watched students apply for ordination in various ecclesiastical groups, I sensed that those seeking ordination in the Episcopal Church were least assured of acceptance for ordination by meeting the educational and professional requirements alone. In a polity that connects the church mainly by pastoral functions, a great deal depends on having a clergy that responds to admonition and persuasion and that symbolically embodies the ethos that characterizes the church. This can place emphasis on the temperament (or spirituality) of the candidate more than on scholarly acumen or prophetic zeal.

Just as bishops can take little action without consultation with various committees, so rectors—although charged with directing the spiritual life of a parish—can do little (other than in matters of liturgy) without the approval of the vestry. The vestry is a group of laypersons that manages the temporal affairs of the parish. The canon specifies that vestries shall be chosen and maintained to meet the legal requirements of the political jurisdictions in which they are formed, since "the Vestry shall be agents and legal representatives of the Parish in all matters concerning its corporate property and the relation of the Parish to its Clergy."[6]

---

6. *Constitution and Canons*, 1997 (title I, canon 14, sec. 2).

Unlike churches that have more than one body concerned with parish affairs—one concerned with worship and spiritual affairs, another with finance and buildings, and perhaps another to deal with social and charitable outreach—the Episcopal Church divides the governance of the parish between the rector, who is in charge of spiritual matters, and the vestry, which (either by itself or through committees) is in charge of other matters. Because it is the only group officially charged to deal with the local parish and its functions, the vestry can exercise considerable pressure on rectors to conform to its expectations. One of the roles bishops may have to perform is to mediate between rectors and vestries when tensions arise because of disagreements, though not a great deal can be done if the situation becomes overly confrontational.

Although there is one bishop in charge of each diocese, that bishop may be assisted in episcopal functions by other episcopally consecrated persons. The diocese may have one or more assistant bishops, who can be appointed *pro temp* to help with episcopal functions such as confirmations and parish visitations. The appointment of assistant bishops must be made from among those duly consecrated to the episcopal office, and such appointments can be withdrawn at any time. The diocese may also elect a suffragan bishop by a similar procedure to that used to elect the bishop. A suffragan bishop has the same sacerdotal powers as the bishop and may step in temporarily as the ecclesiastical authority of the diocese (if, for instance, the bishop dies or is temporarily unable to exercise the normal duties); the suffragan bishop does not have the right of succession to the bishop. The diocese may also elect a bishop coadjutor, done only when a bishop indicates the intention to relinquish the office in the foreseeable future. The coadjutor has the right to succeed as bishop of the diocese.

The election of bishops (and also suffragans and coadjutors) is often a highly politicized process. A committee can nominate three to six persons from names suggested by interested supporters. This gives the diocese knowledge of the candidates and furnishes ample opportunity for candidates to become known by the people they will serve. There is much interest in the electoral process; a process takes place that is akin to electioneering. Candidates' backgrounds, personalities, attitudes, and commitments are ex-

plored. The race is open, and the outcome, determined by vote of
the diocesan convention (voting separately by lay and clergy mem-
berships), uncertain. This is the place in Episcopal polity where
the people take their most active role in determining the direction
the church in their diocese will follow. Persons who lose elections
in one diocese often will be nominated in a different diocese,
where they are not infrequently elected.

After the diocese has voted, the name of the person elected
must be submitted for approval to the other bishops (acting in consultation with their standing committees) for concurrence, or, if
three months or less before a meeting of the General Convention,
to that body. This provision helps to guard the connectionalism
of the Episcopal Church, though it does not insure that all new
bishops are of a single persuasion. Since bishops are consecrated
for life, although they must retire at seventy-two, many bishops
readily approved at one time may find themselves at odds with
the trends in a subsequent period.

Unlike monarchical episcopacy, which can insure conformity
to the ongoing agenda and expectations of the church through
tight hierarchical control of selections, pastoral episcopacy gives
wide latitude for different styles and agendas to develop in ecclesiastical units. Although provisions exist in the canons for the
trial of bishops, trials are for serious moral offenses or a flagrant
repudiation of the church's jurisdiction. As a matter of experience, bishops are seldom tried. They are quite free in their role as
leaders, particularly with respect to the way they interpret faith
and doctrine. They are more similar in the way they carry out
governance and liturgical and ceremonial practices than in their
theology.

The highest office in the American church is that of *presiding
bishop*. The presiding bishop is elected for nine years (the term
used to be twelve) by the General Convention from at least three
candidates proposed by a nominating committee, although the
term is shortened if the presiding bishop reaches sixty-five before
the nine years have passed. This title is significant in that it indicates no hierarchical superiority above that of ordinary bishops.
The presiding bishop presides over the House of Bishops and the
Executive Council, which acts on behalf of the General Conven-

tion between its meetings. Whoever serves in this role facilitates the collegiality among bishops but does not exercise a command authority. The constitution describes the presiding bishop as "the chief pastor of the church." The role is that of a facilitator, an educator, a parliamentarian, a spokesperson for the church as a whole. The presiding bishop travels from diocese to diocese as an instrument and symbol of the church's connectedness. A chancellor, a lay or clergy member of the church, is appointed by the presiding bishop to help carry on the duties of the office.

The rubric *pastoral episcopacy*, which describes this form of church governance, points to an important function of the bishop with respect to the clergy. When things function as they should, the clergy can turn to the bishop for advice, support, counsel, and professional reinforcement. One of the problems with ministry is that it is often a lonely calling. The minister can be thrust into unique roles and entrusted with confidences that are burdensome to bear alone. To seek counsel from members of one's own congregation is often unwise, to seek help from the local ministerial association often more so. Polities in which the oversight function is exercised by peers are not geared to maintaining confidentiality.

When there is rapport and respect between a bishop and members of the clergy, there is a high possibility of discreet and healing support. If there is little or no such rapport, then the clergyperson's position can be difficult. Since bishops are not likely to change— they are active in the same diocese until retirement—there is little recourse for a disgruntled (or maltreated) clergyperson but to relocate to a more cordial diocese. But such relocation may be difficult if there is tension with the existing bishop. The clergyperson seeking to move does not have an inherent claim to standing within the new diocese where he or she must be accepted. The bishops of the diocese to which the clergyperson seeks to move will most likely consult with the bishop in the diocese where the clergyperson has had little rapport so the cause of the tension is not likely to be overlooked.

Pastoral episcopacy differs decisively from monarchical and managerial episcopacy in establishing the pastoral relationship between a priest and a congregation. A "call" procedure rather than an "appointive" process is employed in choosing rectors.

This means that, when a parish ministry ends by resignation, re-tirement, or death, individual parishes—unless they are mission centers supported by the diocese, rather than parishes that raise their own budgets—are free to search for new leadership in a process that resembles that of many nonepiscopal traditions. The process is an open courtship rather than an arranged marriage. The bishop must be notified of the selections, and the new rector must establish canonical residency within the diocese in which the parish is located; the bishop, however, has a consultative rather than a controlling role in the process. The bishop is likely to be heard with great respect if he or she indicates that the choice is not wise, but the fundamental process of selection in the Amer-ican church lies with the parish rather than the diocese. (The Church of England and some Episcopal churches in the Third World operate with something closer to an appointive system). This makes the movement of priests in the Episcopal Church in the United States different from the movement of clergy in Roman Catholic and Methodist denominations. It also means that Episcopal clergy are associated more intimately with and de-pendently upon their local parishes than clergy whose destiny is controlled by ecclesiastical officials having power of appointment (and removal).

The Centrality of Liturgy

The dominant ethos in the Episcopal Church is shaped by wor-ship according to the *Book of Common Prayer*. Although there are different ways to use this book—marked by differences in things like celebrating the Eucharist at an altar against the wall or at a table, calling priests "father" or addressing them less formally, singing rather than reciting the services—there is a distinct pat-tern to the worship that carries over from parish to parish. Some congregations prefer the more traditional tone of so-called Rite I; others prefer the more contemporary Rite II. Some conduct ser-vices in both forms to satisfy different desires within the same congregation. Some congregations alternate the main Sunday ser-vice between Morning Prayer and the Eucharist; others have the Eucharist at all services.

As long as the parish has a priest available, it will most likely celebrate the Eucharist during at least one Sunday service and at other services during the week. The numerous services in the local church provide for a variety of expectations and inclinations as to liturgical practice and such mundane matters as timing. Numerous services also mean that a small sanctuary can take care of a large congregation. The drawback of multiple services is that many churches develop two or more separate or nearly separate congregations and do not develop the congregation-wide cohesiveness that marks churches in which all members attend one weekly service. Another possible drawback is that small congregations owning large sanctuaries seldom see them filled to capacity. Meager occupancy is not conducive to exciting celebration.

In keeping with the observation that the church connects through a book of liturgical forms that makes worship a common experience, the church does not insist on one doctrinal explanation of the Eucharist. Those who hold a high view of the real presence of Christ in the consecrated elements partake alongside those who think of the Eucharist in more commemorative terms. The first set of words as the communicant receives the bread and wine in Rite I suggests both views. "The body of our Lord Jesus Christ, which was given for thee, preserve thy body and soul unto everlasting life." (Those words are consistent with the view of the elements as the actual body of Christ.) "Take and eat this in remembrance that Christ died for thee, and feed on him in thy heart by faith with thanksgiving." (These words are acceptable to those holding the commemorative view.)

Interestingly, this openness about the theory of the Eucharist does not diminish its symbolic significance for the majority of communicants. Common liturgical practice and not doctrinal agreement carries the meaning and provides the common experience. Episcopal practice provides a fascinating illustration of how a community can be cohesive and still tolerate difference of opinion as to the import of faith statements.

While one hears occasional stories of Episcopal priests who love the liturgy rather than strongly believe certain ideas about God—who perhaps have doubts about the nature or reality of

God—these may be apocryphal and are exceptions to the general pattern. They contain a bit of truth, however, because they suggest how great doctrinal differences can be within Episcopalianism. Even the bishops hold different views of the viability of traditional Christian belief. Some are doctrinally conservative, others are radically revisionary in their theological ideas and understandings.

To be sure, the prayer book contains a section of historical documents. This includes the preface to the first (1549) *Book of Common Prayer;* the thirty-nine articles of religion, used as a doctrinal statement in the early Church of England; and an action of the American House of Bishops in 1886 and 1888 affirming an Episcopal quadrilateral as the basis for the church's theology. The thirty-nine articles are a staunchly Calvinistic interpretation of Christian doctrine, including (in article 17) a fairly unequivocal statement about predestination and election. When Episcopalians chide Presbyterians for holding such ideas, it creates quite a conversation to have them read that article.

One realizes, though, that these historical ideas about theological matters do not, as is the case in many other denominations, demand agreement as a precondition of belonging to the Episcopal Church. As for the Episcopal quadrilateral, it differs from the Methodist version of scripture, tradition, reason, and experience. It refers to scripture as containing all things necessary to salvation, the creeds (Apostolic and Nicene), baptism and Eucharist, and the historical episcopate (apostolic ministry).

Episcopalians considered as a group do not push rigorously for doctrinal closure or for complete agreement about the moral dimensions of Christian fidelity. This has kept the church from dividing over irresolvable differences of opinion. Confronted with the question of whether holding slaves was compatible with Christian discipleship, the Episcopal Church allowed individuals and individual dioceses to treat the matter locally. This meant that, whereas several mainline denominations split over this issue into northern and southern branches, the Episcopal Church stayed united. Before ordaining women as priests came to be generally accepted, the church allowed individual bishops to follow their own consciences. Recently, bishops have been mandated to accept woman as clergy within their dioceses, which has not been greeted without grumbling. In the present controversy over sexual orientation, there seemingly is less willingness to make a definitive judgment than there has been in some past controversies. Each side seems to want its position vindicated.

Interestingly, although the Episcopal Church has a carefully selected, specially (apostolically) ordained, and clearly professional clergy, it involves laypersons—not only in governance in the ways mentioned—but in its liturgies (particularly those celebrated weekly). This contrasts with the practice of many churches in offering a seemingly less elevated theory of the ministry. The lessons (except for the Gospel) are usually read by laity as are the prayers of the people. Laypersons help serving the wine (not the bread) in the Eucharist. Persons, at the request of the rector or priest in charge, are licensed to perform these tasks by the bishop of the diocese. The stipulated period of service is not to exceed three years, subject to renewal. Lay readers can preach with the special authorization of the bishop. Many years ago (but still within my memory), lay readers were expected to read prepared sermons rather than compose their own.

The relative weight between preaching and celebration is evidenced in the fact that ministers from other denominations, with agreement from the bishop, may preach, but they may not celebrate the Eucharist. This stricture is not followed absolutely, and a concordat between Lutherans and Episcopalians has recently opened both churches to celebrations of the Eucharist by clergy of either denomination. (A similar concordat legitimizes interchange between Lutherans and several Reformed bodies, but as yet no bridge has been built between Episcopalians and the Reformed groups.)

The Episcopal Church offers a rich amalgam. It offers intellectual understanding of the faith, though in selecting clergy intellectual acumen is not the primary quality sought. It offers organizational connectedness, but the church is held together more by participation in a common ethos than by strict obedience to rules or a required moral conformity. Finally, it offers liturgical richness that involves people in a variety of richly satisfying roles.

Governance in Orthodox Churches

The casual observer might expect that governance in the Orthodox churches would be similar to that in Roman Catholicism. Both have a long tradition; both are considered catholic in nature; both have, at times, been officially established in their respective political sovereignties; both are highly liturgical in their practice; and both have monastic orders. But such an inference based on similarities in history and practice becomes misleading if applied to governance. The governance of the Orthodox churches for centuries has resembled the pastoral model, although there is enough difference to make another more accurate. Many authors point out that governance in the Orthodox Church has long been more like what now characterizes the Episcopal Church than like governance in the contemporary Roman Catholic Church.[7]

Those who describe governance in the Orthodox churches often start by indicating how Orthodoxy repudiated the monarchical model. According to Methodios Fouyas, "While the Roman Church is monarchical and authoritarian, the structure of the Orthodox Church is hierarchical and conciliar. The Orthodox Church admits that each particular Church, in both the East and the West, is self-governing, and that they were so in the time of the undivided church."[8]

This means that the role of the Orthodox bishop is symbolic and nurturing rather than controlling. This in no way diminishes the spiritual importance of the bishop's role. Indeed, the bishop, who is a monastic, is seen as the embodiment of the tradition— one who exemplifies in a special way through his presence and behavior the faith and piety of the church. The role of the bishop and the life of the church cannot be separated.[9] Nevertheless the laity of the church are deeply involved in its governance and even in shaping its life and thought.

---

7. See Nicolas Zernov, *Orthodox Encounter* (London: James Clarke, 1961), 50.

8. Methodios Fouyas, *Orthodoxy, Roman Catholicism, and Anglicanism* (London: Oxford University Press, 1972), 151.

9. See Lawrence Cross, *Eastern Christianity: The Byzantine Tradition* (Sydney and Philadelphia: E. J. Dwyer, 1988), 40–46.

The Orthodox Church is the most democratic system of believers. Her clergy are elected with the approval of the laity, with very rare exceptions. Laymen play an important role in the administration of the Church. They are elected to the Executive Council of the Church, and they have great administrative responsibilities in the local parish. And all believe, all live, all worship, all belong to the same body. All may occupy a significant position, and work accordingly for the well-being of the body of the Church. All are animated by the same principles of spiritual life, the same faith, the same ethics, the same means of sanctification and communion with the Creator and Redeemer, God.[10]

In this unique unity of faith and practice, the role of the clergy, of which there are three categories (deacon, priest, and bishop), has significance. Deacons assist with pastoral functions in local parishes. Priests, who may be married if they have married before ordination, officiate at the sacraments. Bishops, chosen from celibate monastics, provide the link among parishes and a profound symbolic continuity with the tradition.

The role of the laity is equally essential to the function of the church as the people of God. Although hierarchy is present, the church would not be the church without the laity and its participation. Laity are more actively involved in Orthodox leadership than in Catholicism, and they may even be more active than in much of Anglicanism. Lay theologians are common, often serving as advisers to bishops and as professors in theological institutions. Bishops often consult with the laity in arriving at decisions. In a few Orthodox groups, both in the United States and in Europe, rules allow for the participation of laity in the election of bishops. However, the norm is for bishops to be elected by the synods of bishops. Laity must consent to the assignment of priests to their parishes. They bear responsibility for the material needs of the parishes and of other functioning bodies of the church. In this role they make decisions about matters of temporal import, as is true of the vestries in the Episcopal Church.

Canon law is much less extensive in Orthodox ecclesiology than in Roman ecclesiology. There is less pressure for uniformity

---

10. Demetrios J. Constantelos, *The Greek Orthodox Church: Faith, History, and Practice* (New York: Seabury Press, 1967), 100f.

through law. Over its long history, Orthodoxy has seen changes and variations in specific matters related to its governance. It has never departed, however, from the belief that bishops are important for its polity. They are essential, not so much for directing the operation of the church in all the details, as for preserving the spiritual validity of the tradition. The sacraments, which the Orthodox call "the mysteries," constitute the essence of the church's being. It would be inconceivable to think about Orthodoxy without them. A deeply impressive spirituality revolves about the sacraments—a spirituality that nurtures all the human senses rather than merely informing the mind.

Although the patriarch of Constantinople has been something of a symbolic head for the several Orthodox churches—churches that are often organized around geographical or political entities—there has been no centralization of authority in Orthodoxy. Terms like *infallibility* are not used to designate the authority of any person or document. But the church in its holistic function is considered to carry on the work of Christ truly, fully, and dependably. Although the people are indispensable to the church's being, they do not, by themselves, constitute the source of the church's legitimacy, nor do they define the nature of the church by their decisions. In Orthodox practice, the local parish is a key and functioning location for authentic faith and practice, but it is not autonomous as in congregationalism.

Up to the present, Orthodoxy has not been viewed as a mainstream option in American religious life. Adherents have largely been members of groups associated with Orthodoxy before immigrating. But Orthodoxy is coming to be an increasingly visible part of the religious scene in the United States. It is attracting converts who appreciate the catholic richness Orthodoxy offers without the disadvantages they see in monarchical governance.

RESOURCES ON PASTORAL AND EXEMPLARY EPISCOPACY

For Understanding the Episcopal Church

Constitution and Canons for the Government of the Protestant Episcopal Church in the United States of America, Otherwise Known as the Episcopal Church, Together with the Rules of Order. Adopted in General Conventions, 1789–1997. Revised by the 1997 Convention.

Dawley, Powell Mills. *The Episcopal Church and Its Work.* With the collaboration of James Thayer Addison. Greenwich, Conn.: Seabury Press, 1995.

Doe, Norman. *Canon Law in the Anglican Communion: A Worldwide Perspective.* New York: Oxford University Press, 1998.

Krumm, John McGill. *Why I Am an Episcopalian.* New York: Thomas Nelson and Sons, 1957.

Mills, Frederick V., Sr. *Bishops by Ballots: An Eighteenth-Century Ecclesiastical Revolution.* New York: Oxford University Press, 1978.

Moore, Peter, ed. *Bishops: But What Kind? Reflections on Episcopacy.* London: SPCK, 1982.

Pittenger, W. Norman. *The Episcopalian Way of Life.* Englewood Cliffs, N.J.: Prentice-Hall, 1957.

For Understanding the Orthodox Churches

Benz, Ernst. *The Eastern Orthodox Church: Its Thought and Life.* Translated from the German by Richard Winston and Clara Winston. Chicago: Aldine, 1963.

Calian, Samuel Carnegie. *Icon and Pulpit: The Protestant-Orthodox Encounter.* Philadelphia: Westminster Press, 1968.

Constantelos, Demetrios J. *The Greek Orthodox Church: Faith, History, and Practice.* New York: Seabury Press, 1967.

Cross, Lawrence. *Eastern Christianity: The Byzantine Tradition.* Sydney and Philadelphia: E. J. Dwyer, 1988.

Fouyas, Methodios. *Orthodoxy, Roman Catholicism, and Anglicanism.* London: Oxford University Press, 1972.

Meyendorff, John. *Orthodoxy and Catholicity.* New York: Sheed and Ward, 1966.

———. *Vision of Unity.* Crestwood, N.Y.: St. Vladimir's Seminary Press, 1987.

Zernov, Nicolas. *Orthodox Encounter.* London: James Clarke, 1961.

Part Two

GOVERNANCE BY ELDERS, APPOINTEES, AND THE SPIRITUALLY MATURE

4

REPRESENTATIVE ELDERSHIP

THE THREE CHAPTERS in this part of the book discuss ecclesiastical governance by specially designated groups. The most common term for the members of such ruling groups is *elders*, though other terms are also used. The specially designated groups are often laypersons, though, in many forms of eldership, ministers with responsibility for preaching and administering the sacraments have a designated role in governance and are also called elders. In the polity discussed in this chapter, elders are elected by the people. This is the most widespread form of eldership and an important aspect of governance in Presbyterian and Reformed churches. In other cases, those with governance roles (whether or not they are called elders) are appointed by senior officials—often in recognition of long-term allegiance to the traditions and practice of a particular tradition. This pattern will be discussed in chapter 5. In still other cases, examined in chapter 6, the leaders are chosen by nonpolitical means or emerge because they are recognized as having special maturity or wisdom.

GOVERNANCE BY ELDERS

In churches belonging to the Reformed tradition, governance is by elders who are elected by democratic procedures. "Elders" may include young persons as well as seniors, traditionalists as well as persons with more innovative temperaments and, in most current practice, men as well as women. The most highly developed and most clearly functional forms of eldership belong to this elective pattern, which operates in covenanted communities according to constitutional provisions to choose persons for governance responsibilities.

The polity of Presbyterian churches is the prototype of repre-sentative eldership. In Presbyterian polity, ministers of word and sacrament (sometimes referred to as *teaching elders*) share in the governance of the church with elected representatives chosen by the congregations to which they belong (referred to as *ruling elders*). Ruling elders are expressly ordained to their office by laying on of hands in the local church. The ordination is similar in many respects and different only in details from the ordination of persons set apart for the ministry of word and sacrament. Such ordination symbolizes a special dedication to governance, which requires commitment and competency.

Elders exercise their responsibilities according to the guidance of their own nurtured consciences and not merely as spokespersons of particular interest groups. Such persons may rotate in and out of active governance roles by action of the congregation, but their ordained status as elders is continuing and permanent. The group of elders in active service governing the local parish is called the *session*. When serving on the session elders bear responsibility for the spiritual condition of the parish over which they exercise oversight. Any elder, whether on not on the session, can partici-pate in the policy making of the denomination as a whole by being designated as a delegate to a higher judicatory.

The instrument that controls the life of the Presbyterian Church is called *The Book of Order*. This is a fairly long and elaborate doc-ument that specifies how the church is to be governed and how it is to worship. The specific rules for governance in the Presby-terian Church are constantly being changed to provide explicit constitutional guidance for all deliberative bodies. One of the in-teresting features of Presbyterian church life is the preparation of study guides to the *Book of Order* for persons elected to governance roles. Those in governance roles need to learn the polity and to be alert to its provisions. Some laypersons elected to governance roles become especially knowledgeable about the polity of the church, and some achieve high office in the higher judicatories.

In many respects, governance by elders shares with episcopal polities the premise that special gifts are necessary to maintain the tradition and to conduct ecclesiastical affairs according to the cherished phrase, "decently and in order." But this concern about good order is grounded in an equally strong conviction that authority should be exercised by a group of leaders especially designated for that task, rather than by any individual. Elders constitute a group with special concerns and competencies, yet they can provide checks and balances so that no single person—not even the minister—is vested with power that can be exercised unilaterally. Because group decision making is the norm, this polity requires great skill in parliamentary procedure and great patience with the committee process.

Presbyterian polity also calls for the election and ordination of persons as deacons. This, like eldership, is an ordained office, to which ordination confers a standing that lasts for life (or until resigned or nullified by renouncing jurisdiction of the Presbyterian Church). Deacons are primarily responsible for serving the needy, either in the congregation or through the wider church. In the former southern Presbyterian Church, deacons cared for the property and finances of the church, but in current Presbyterian polity these matters are in the hands of the trustees, an unordained office.[1] In the Reformed Church in America, both elders and deacons are members of a single governing board for the local church.

Much of the literature advocating church governance by elders appeals directly to scripture as a warrant. The term *presbyters* is derived from the Greek word for elders. This appeal to scripture as a warrant for presbyterian governance is found primarily in church groups formed during the Protestant Reformation; these are the same groups in which biblical authority is considered the touchstone for theological faith and ecclesiastical practice. Given that Presbyterian polity was worked out in contrast to the prevailing Anglican pattern, perhaps its advocates were under special onus to legitimize it by appeal to scripture more than to tradition.

But there are other reasons why governance by elders commends itself to its practitioners. Most of its forms share with

---

1. There is considerable disagreement as to whether it is wiser to separate the functions of the elders and trustees, or to combine them in a unicameral board so that the financial and logistical aspect of church life is dealt with in light of its spiritual life and gospel imperatives.

episcopacy the concept of *supervisory connectionalism*—that is, a process by which local congregations are subject to considerable control by higher (or more widely exercised) ecclesiastical authority. Presbyterianism has historically been as uneasy about what in earlier days was called *independency* as it has been with episcopacy. Although such connectionalism maintains common features in the life and thought of churches, it also becomes the source of parliamentary maneuvering whenever the church deals with controversial matters.

When major theological differences arise or when there are great disagreements about what constitutes legitimate moral practice, negotiating common ground within a connectional polity that functions by a representative process can require great forbearance and reconciling skills. This polity generally makes it impossible to sweep disagreement under the rug of sanctimoniousness or to deal with it under the protective curtain of pastoral admonition. Divisions probably occur more frequently in churches governed by group deliberation than in churches with bishops, more because the battles have to be fought openly than because the members are inherently more cantankerous.

Because presbyterian polity is heavily connectional, it creates a carefully and widely recognized denominational identity. Although the separation of church and state has rendered the idea of established religions inapplicable in the United States, presbyterian polity enables denominations so governed to function as official establishments in much the same way as churches with bishops. Thus, in England, the established church is governed by bishops; in Scotland, by presbyters. Churches thus established can perform public functions and take stands on public matters in ways that carry a presumption of official weight.

The most useful image for polities in this group is that of a commonwealth—an image that offers a distinct contrast with hierarchy and, significantly, with participatory democracy. Commonwealths vest authority in the people but are marked by a strong covenantal agreement to pursue the common good. Elders who rule are chosen by the people, not without regard for the positions they hold on matters of controversy, but more often (and in theory more importantly) for their personal stature than their policy stances. They are accorded respect and consequently are expected to use their good judgment. Eldership is premised more on "wisdomship" than on partisanship.

In presbyterian polities, governance is shared by ministers of word and sacrament (who are examined and ordained by presbyteries) and ruling elders (laypersons set apart by ordination by local congregations but bearing responsibilities for decision making in the denomination as a whole). Parity between these two groups of elders is carefully maintained to insure that the church is neither governed clerically nor radically altered by upsurges of lay pressure. However, Presbyterian governance has never employed the concept of concurrent majorities between lay and clerical groups in joint deliberations. Members of deliberative bodies constitute one decision-making group, in which the voices and votes of clergy and lay elders in equal numbers are mingled without distinction.

THE ROLE OF THE PRESBYTERY

The governance structure of presbyterianism consists of several decision-making levels, which interact in many particulars. The most pivotal and significant deliberative body is the *presbytery* (or, in the Reformed Church of America, the *classis*). This geographically defined body consists of all ministers who reside within it plus an equal number of governing elders from area churches. (If there are more ministers than churches, the number of ruling elders increases comparably.) The presbytery is not an association of congregations that owes its identity or standing to the member churches, but it is the body by which congregations are established, legitimized, and monitored. The presbytery has supervisory power over all denominational activity within its bounds—which means it performs the functions that bishops have in episcopal polities.

In many respects, the presbytery exercises such supervisory functions with greater specificity than many bishops, particularly those in the Episcopal Church in the United States. Although ministers and churches come together through a call system, the presbytery has veto power over the establishment of all such pastoral relationships—even over temporary (stated) supply pastors for vacant churches. Presbyterian ministers who undertake religious work within a presbytery are expected to have the presbytery's approval and are expected to show that such ministry conforms to the denomination's practices and norms. If they undertake religious work in a removed area (termed "laboring out of bounds"), ministers are expected to have permission both from the presbytery of which they are members and the presbytery within which such work occurs. The presbytery in which the minister holds membership usually checks with the second presbytery to be sure the arrangement is satisfactory.

Strictly speaking, the Lord's Supper is not to be celebrated outside the local parish—where such celebration is authorized by the session—without the approval of the presbytery. In Presbyterian practice, elders serve the elements (bread and unfermented grape juice) to persons in the pews, though other ways of celebrating the Lord's Supper are not constitutionally prohibited. In theory, ministers of word and sacrament do not have power to decide when (or how) the worship life of the congregation will be carried out. That decision is in the hands of the session.

The presbytery's control over its clergy is specific and detailed and starts with the first steps to ordained ministry. The presbytery accepts persons thinking about ordination (called inquirers) very early in their path to the ministry. It accepts recommendations from the person's session and examines them at the beginning for spiritual experience and motives for seeking to enter the ministry. They may initially share with a committee their reasons for being ordained, but they must appear before the entire presbytery membership and be accepted by the entire body. Then the presbytery (sometimes delegating the specifics to a committee) takes over their preparation for the ministry, exercising concern about their choice of seminary and curricular selections. The approval of presbytery is required for any deviation from standard educational requirements, and while the national church administers standardized examinations for persons nearing the end of their seminary education, any presbytery can accept or reject a candidate irrespective of the results.

When the preparation is complete, the Committee on Preparation for Ministry certifies that a candidate is ready to receive a call. After the candidate receives a call, the presbytery in which the call is located examines candidates prior to ordination to determine their adherence to confessional standards. This is done on the floor of presbytery, and any member can pose a question. Presbyteries vary in the degree to which they insist on doctrinal correctness, though doctrinal stances are generally the focus of attention in such examinations. Even ordained ministers wishing to change membership from one presbytery to another will often be asked questions about their theological stance, and a presbytery can deny membership even if the person is in good standing in their present membership (such denial rarely happens, however). Ordination to minister of word and sacrament, which is generally done in the person's own church or in the church to which the person is called, occurs in one step. Presbyterian polity has only one ministerial rank or category.

Through its Committee on Ministry, the presbytery guides local congregations in searching for pastors when there is a vacancy, and the presbytery as a whole examines all ministers for theological soundness before it approves a call and installs a pastor. The services of ordination (if required) and of installation, which occur in the church where the minister is to pastor, are important formal aspects of the Presbyterian ethos. All members of the presbytery can be present to participate in the "laying on of hands," by which ordination is conferred, or in the welcome given to those already ordained. In most cases, the attending clergy wear robes and process as a body. This symbolizes their power as a body to carry on the apostolic tradition. In an important sense, the action signifies a role that is a corporate equivalent to that of individual bishops in other polities.

Presbyteries meet more often than many corresponding bodies in other denominations. The meetings may be monthly (though not usually in summers, or in the month containing Holy Week), and the presbytery is subject to a called meeting if a matter needs attention between stated meetings. Each presbytery elects its presiding officer, called a *moderator*, for one year. The moderator may be either a minister or a ruling elder and, as a matter of historical practice, the office moves from one to the other frequently. The moderator chairs the meetings of presbytery (and sees that all goes "decently and in order").

In addition to the moderator, who serves a short term, the presbytery usually has two ongoing offices. The *stated clerk* is the parliamentarian, who is responsible for keeping the moderator and presbytery members straight about procedure. The stated clerk also gathers and preserves the records of the presbytery and completes the reports required by higher judicatories of the church. The stated clerk—who may be full- or part-time—is elected for a five-year term, but can succeed himself or herself and usually serves a long tenure. Presbyteries also have a *treasurer,* who keeps the financial affairs in order.

Another position with a continuing relationship to the presbytery is an *executive* (or general) *presbyter.* This is a functional rather than a constitutionally specified role, and it is not required. The executive presbyter functions in ways that bear resemblance to duties of the pastoral bishop—though many of them would resist the analogy. They can function as general facilitators of the work of the presbytery. This may involve administration, but it often includes pastoral care of the presbytery's clergy members. A general or executive presbyter can deal with problems within the presbytery without necessarily making them public (though this function is limited). The executive presbyter can also stay abreast of the work and program of the national church and interpret it to the presbytery. The executive presbyter can meet the demands of an emergency (such as preaching on short notice in the case of sickness or death of a minister).

When performed with skill, sensitivity, and imagination, the work of the presbytery executive can make a considerable difference in the presbytery. At times, however, tensions can develop between the executive presbyter and the stated clerk (unless, as is occasionally true, both offices, and rarely also that of treasurer, are held by the same person). In any event, it is hard to specify the "head" of the presbytery—even as it is hard to specify the "head" of a genuine commonwealth. The leadership is not undesignated; it is divided among several persons, all of whom are responsible to the presbytery as a deliberative body and who exercise key roles in facilitating the presbytery's function.

LOCAL PARISHES

On the parish level, a group of ruling elders constitutes the *session* (*consistory* in the Reformed Church in America). This is the governing body of the local parish. The meetings of the session must be conducted by a minister of word and sacrament, who can act in this role only by designation of the presbytery—a designation integral to the office of pastors and specifically assigned in other cases, such as in vacant churches. The minister is called a moderator when functioning in this way. The minister of a church works in conjunction with the session to determine all the church's activities, and in theory the minister has no power, apart from a role on the session, to determine how things will be done. This is the case in the church's liturgical and theological functions as well as in its logistical affairs and outreach programs. In the informing model, the minister of word and sacrament is a teacher who instructs the local church about faith and practice and who accomplishes tasks only by pedagogical persuasion, which prepares the session to see that its decisions accord with the practices of the denomination as guided by scripture and the historical creeds.

The activities of every church are monitored by the presbytery, which annually reads the minutes of session meetings of every church and meticulously ferrets out failure to follow constitutional requirements. For instance, one requirement stipulates that every meeting open with prayer. Woe to the church whose minutes do not indicate that a prayer was said. But there are many other stipulations about proper practice.

In addition, the presbytery's Committee on the Ministry (or its designees) visits each church at least once every three years; the local church is required to submit statistics annually to the presbytery (through the stated clerk) regarding membership and financial affairs. The presbytery controls the acquisition and the disposition of all property held in trust for the denomination, and property cannot be used apart from that function. The presbytery must approve all actions that affect the status of properties— for example, mortgaging, selling, or major renovation. If churches withdraw from the denomination, they lose their property (though exceptions are sometimes allowed). No change in the conditions of a minister's call (employment) can be made without the church reporting it to the presbytery and obtaining approval. Every aspect of a minister's relationship to a local church is a concern of the presbytery and known to all its members.

HIGHER GOVERNING BODIES

The higher governing bodies of the church derive their membership from the presbyteries, which elect delegates. The highest governing body is the General Assembly, which meets annually and consists of an equal number of ministers and laypersons (that is, teaching elders and ruling elders). The work done each year by the General Assembly is detailed and wide-ranging (those who attend usually say "exhausting").

The docket of the General Assembly is carefully drawn in advance and ranges over many matters, such as constitutional provisions governing the church, doctrinal matters, organizational logistics for the church's operations, finances, social-witness resolutions, and mission strategy. Any presbytery or elected commissioner (i.e., delegate member) can overture the General Assembly to consider a matter of concern. Numerous overtures are made to each General Assembly, sorted according their subject, assigned to a committee, and reported back with recommendations (for, against, or with modifications, as the committee decides). Assignment to the standing committees of General Assemblies (that is, the committees that come into and go out of existence with the assembly that forms them) are now made by random selection—assisted by computer. Except for the chairperson, members are not selected for particular competency or a record of advocacy on particular issues. The agenda, called dockets, of deliberative bodies are drawn up with time slots allotted for each item, and if deliberations on the floor are not completed in the time given, discussions are often postponed to the end of the meeting. (If only academic faculties would take note!)

Some overtures seek changes in the church's constitution or form of government. For these to become effective as definitions of church polity, the General Assembly must adopt the overture (either as submitted or as revised) and send it to the presbyteries for their concurrence or rejection. If a majority of the presbyteries concur, the next General Assembly declares the constitutional change effective. This means that on major matters affecting the fundamental governance of the denomination, the General Assembly has a pivotal but not decisive power. However, it is not unusual for presbyteries to overture a General Assembly to enact legislation on procedural matters and even with specific legislative objectives. Even minor matters are frequently dealt with by overtures requiring a constitutional change. The result is that the specifics of governance are constantly changing and become quite lengthy.

On other matters, however, General Assemblies act by majority vote, and the actions become church policy. This is the case with programs, budgets, and pronouncements on social witness. Such decisions cover many aspects of the church's operations and its policy on issues of moral and public import, but they do not become aspects of its constituting order and are subject to change by subsequent General Assemblies.

There is an intermediate governing body between the presbytery and the General Assembly. It is called a *synod* and also consists of teaching and ruling elders in equal numbers, elected by the presbyteries. Synods cover larger geographical areas than presbyteries—usually four or five states. They meet at least annually, as does the General Assembly, and some meet more frequently. Synods do not deal with constitutional matters, so their function is primarily to advance the mission and program of the church's life in their given region—which often includes arranging for the support of educational institutions within their boundaries.

The office of *moderator* of General Assembly has considerable symbolic significance. The person elected to this position presides at the meeting of the General Assembly that elects him or her and travels widely throughout the church in the year that follows, speaking to various groups and representing the church in other ecclesiastical settings. The election of the moderator has many features of an open political contest, with the nominees making their views known prior to the meeting and appearing at open forums. The focus is primarily on matters of policy even though their role does not give them special capacity to determine the church's actions. Any elder, whether a layperson or a minister, can be elected to this high office, and one of the fascinating aspects of Presbyterian life is the wide diversity of persons who serve in this role—lay and ministerial, male and female, white and ethnically diverse, relatively young and obviously senior.

Another fascinating aspect is how, in times of considerable disagreement about policy, a General Assembly will decide one way and then, at the same meeting, elect a moderator who advocated the defeated position. Moderators of local presbyteries and of synods are similarly elected to one-year terms, but they do not have the visibility (or the travel schedule) of the moderator of the General Assembly. The retiring moderator gives a sermon at the opening service of the General Assembly that ends her or his time in office. When the moderator of the General Assembly is a minister of word and sacrament, he or she can officiate at the Lord's Supper as celebrated there, but when a layperson is moderator she or he asks a minister to do so.

The office of *stated clerk* plays a very important role in the church. As is the case with presbyteries, the stated clerk of the General Assembly serves for a longer term than the moderator—five years rather than one. The term is renewable for as long as the electing body wishes to have the individual serve. The stated clerk is the parliamentarian and record keeper for the denomination. The stated clerk sees that all actions are in conformity with constitutional requirements, collects data on churches from presbyteries, and sees that the minutes of the General Assembly are properly prepared and publicly available. Astute and able persons often are elected to such positions, and, in many cases, their abilities become somewhat awesome through practice. The stated clerk often affects the parliamentary process by which a judicatory makes decisions even more decisively than the moderator, but can only act through the deliberative process of the judicatory and not as a policy maker. When the church is called to take an action or to make a public witness between meetings of the General Assembly, the stated clerk (usually in consultation or conjunction with the Moderator) does what is called for—such as writing to a public official about a pressing social issue—though such actions seldom attract the degree of public attention as do statements by ecclesiastical officials who wear miters.

DOCTRINE AND WORSHIP

Doctrine plays an important role in the Reformed tradition. The churches in this tradition define their identity by their doctrinal positions far more than by their liturgical practices. This is the case even with the Reformed Church in America, whose constitution includes official liturgies mandated for many occasions as well as sections dealing with governance and faith.[2] (Not all pastors in that denomination follow such liturgies as fully as the polity presumes.) Although the faith of some groups with presbyterian governance has in the past been defined by a single creed, today in the Presbyterian Church USA *The Book of Confessions* consists of eleven confessional statements, covering many years and circumstances. All eleven are included to give historical continuity to the church's witness and to include recent examples of the importance of grounding the Christian life in theological confession. By including all eleven creeds, the Presbyterian Church makes it clear that creedal instruments are subordinate to scripture in matters of doctrine, although Presbyterians differ widely in how they read scripture, just as they differ in accepting a particular aspect of any of the eleven creeds. The way in which Presbyterians highlight and affirm the relation of scripture to tradition is to require persons to indicate that they accept the creeds as indicative of the system of doctrine in scripture rather than as propositions binding in and of themselves.

The attempt to define a church confessionally is no guarantee of conformity. It simply tends to focus differences around theological questions rather than liturgical practice. However, sharp disagreements sometimes occur about specific moral stances. At times, Presbyterians have come to a parting of the ways—that

---

2. See the discussion of the difference between constitutions of the Presbyterian Church and the Reformed Church in America, with regard to provisions for liturgy, in Daniel J. Meeter, *Meeting Each Other in Doctrine, Liturgy, and Government: The Bicentennial of the Celebration of the Constitution of the Reformed Church in America* (Grand Rapids, Mich.: Eerdmans, 1993).

is, to church division. They are less likely than Episcopalians, for example, to accept diversity in theological stances and moral practice. Meanwhile, the church keeps wrestling with issues on which there is no consensus. It is possible that if the differences cannot be reconciled, they will become the occasion for division—as they have in the past. One of the most serious debates in the contemporary Presbyterian Church is whether the seemingly irresoluble disagreement about the legitimacy of ordaining practicing homosexuals to offices in the church calls for a new parting. This is a particularly vexing matter for Presbyterians, since both lay and clergy forms of leadership require ordination, and conditions restricting ordination of certain groups affect a much larger number of persons than when such restrictions apply only to clergy. As of this writing, instead of having decided some of the questions related to sexuality, the church has put a two-year suspension on legislation involving such matters. Only time will tell whether this action leads to steps that begin to resolve the problem, or whether it becomes the occasion of a new division. Meanwhile, conservatives on this issue feel that nothing has yet been lost, and liberals that nothing has yet been gained.

A little-realized fact about Presbyterian and Reformed churches is that most have a book of liturgies, with such titles as *A Book of Common Worship* (American), *A Book of Common Order* (Scottish), or *A Book of Services* (The United Reformed Church in England). It is jokingly said that these are provided for voluntary disuse. Although the language of these books is as theologically rich and the prose as stately as that in the service manuals of any denomination, they do not provide the basis for a uniform worship practice. This may be because the Presbyterians prefer to depend on the directions given in the Directory for Worship—a part of *The Book of Order*. The statement about the corporate worship of God found in the Directory for Worship captures well the Presbyterian understanding of this important function.

> For the right ordering of corporate worship the Church is obliged to remember both that people are to stand fast in the liberty to which Christ has set them free, and that all things are to be done decently and in order. Public worship need not follow prescribed

form, but careless public worship may be both an offense to God and a stumbling block to his people.

Those responsible for the ordering of public worship of God should maintain fidelity to the aspects of public worship which are seen in the Scripture, and in the New Testament Church; maintain receptiveness to the historic experience of Christendom, appropriating for their own such elements from the past as have been found consistent with the right showing forth of the gospel; and in the light of these resources of Scripture, and ecumenical experience, endeavor to serve the needs and situations of their own worshipping community.[3]

The spirituality of the Reformed tradition has tended to emphasize heartfelt prayer, composed for particular occasions, and has fostered the articulation of special needs and petitions. Many persons in the Reformed tradition feel that precomposed prayers, such as found in worship books, cannot achieve this desired consequence. A minority, put off by the not infrequent casualness of extemporaneous utterance, feel otherwise, and they use the *Book of Common Worship* in order to avoid sloppiness. There is increasing use of the lectionary in the denomination's churches. In most churches, the pastoral prayer is as important an aspect of the service as a well-thought-out and scholarly sermon.

The Presbyterian (Reformed) pattern of governance by elders is a major alternative to both episcopal and congregational polities. It is a highly refined and deeply cherished form of governance which many have suffered adversity to defend. Its strength lies in the high participation it requires by those charged with its maintenance and utilization. Its possible limitation is that it can become somewhat legalized and that it offers guidance for the mind more adequately than succor for the feelings. As one guidebook to patterns of church life aptly puts it, the Presbyterian Church is "more cerebral and verbal than emotional and aesthetic; it values understanding, learning, and propriety."[4]

---

3. This wording is taken from the *Book of Order, 1978–79*, chap. 4, par. 1. The corresponding section in the *Book of Order, 1998–99* (chap. 3, par. 1 and 2), does not alter the emphasis on balancing freedom and order, but it stresses the authority of the Holy Spirit speaking in and through Scripture. It is more prosaic.

4. Frank S. Mead and Samuel S. Hill, *Handbook of Denominations in the United States*, new 10th ed. (Nashville: Abingdon Press, 1995), 247.

Resources on Representative Eldership

For Understanding the Presbyterian Church

Alston, Wallace M., Jr. *The Church.* Atlanta: John Knox Press, 1984.

Beattie, Frank A. *Companion to the Constitution: Polity for the Local Church.* 4th ed. Louisville: Geneva Press, 1999.

Book of Common Worship. Prepared by the Theology and Worship Ministry of the Presbyterian Church, U.S.A. Louisville: Westminster/John Knox Press, 1993.

Constitution of the Presbyterian Church, U.S.A., Part One: The Book of Confessions. Louisville: Office of General Assembly, 1998–99. *Part Two: The Book of Order.* Louisville: Office of General Assembly, 1998–99.

Hall, David W., and Joseph H. Hall, eds. *Paradigms in Polity.* Grand Rapids, Mich.: Eerdmans, 1994.

Hart, D. G., and Mark A. Noll, eds. *Dictionary of the Presbyterian and Reformed Tradition in America.* Downers Grove, Ill.: Intervarsity Press, 1999.

Leith, John H. *The Church: A Believing Fellowship.* Atlanta: John Knox Press, 1965.

For Understanding the Reformed Church in America

Book of Church Order: Including the Government, the Disciplinary Procedures, the Bylaws and Rules of Order of the General Synod, the Reformed Church in America. New York: Reformed Church Press, 1997.

Hageman, Howard G. *Our Reformed Church.* New York: Board of Education, Reformed Church in America, 1963.

Hoff, Marvin D. *Structure for Mission: The Reformed Church in America.* Grand Rapids, Mich.: Eerdmans, 1985.

Meeter, Daniel J. *Meeting Each Other in Doctrine, Liturgy, and Government: The Bicentennial of the Celebration of the Constitution of the Reformed Church in America.* Grand Rapids, Mich.: Eerdmans, 1993.

5

Leadership by Appointment and Seniority

R EPRESENTATIONAL ELDERSHIP as it operates in presbyterian governance bears close affinity to democratic governance insofar as the elders are selected, almost always by election, for their roles. It makes most decisions by the parliamentary deliberation of its elders, following open discussion.

There are other church polities in which decisions are made by a leadership group but that differ significantly from representative eldership, primarily because the determination of official roles is by a designation process that—whether by deliberate design or by customary practice—is essentially nonpolitical. Interestingly, these forms of designated leadership are generally found in churches that either eliminate the role of clergy or downplay its special or professional significance. Such forms of governance are evident in groups with widely differing beliefs and practices, though in most of them the Christian life is a matter of complete and intense commitment expected equally of all members.

This chapter examines governance in the Church of Jesus Christ of Latter-day Saints (Mormons). The governance of this church is highly controlled; it is authoritarian rather than democratic. Those on top appoint most of the lesser officials while they themselves come into governance by fidelity and influence and, at the very top, strictly by seniority.

The Mormons have been involved in much controversy over the years about their beliefs and practices. Their elevation of the Book of Mormon to a status equal to the Bible has not been honored outside their own constituency. Their (now abandoned) practice of polygamy was strongly opposed and even prosecuted by civil authorities. The long-standing, but recently abrogated, exclusion of Afro-Americans from its priesthood has also been a matter for which the Mormons have been criticized. Questions have been raised concerning where to place it among ecclesiastical groups. Arthur C. Piepkorn does not include it in his monumental and extensive treatment of major religious groups.[1] It has been said that it is neither Catholic nor Protestant.[2] In February 2001, the leadership took action to emphasize the Christian identity of the Church of Jesus Christ of Latter-day Saints, urging people to call it by its full name and in subsequent references to use the phrase "The Church of Jesus Christ."[3] Whatever its theological identity, the Church of Jesus Christ of Latter-day Saints furnishes a unique and instructive variation of church governance.

The governance of the Church of Jesus Christ of Latter-day Saints is extremely complex. A chart showing the various offices is full of interlocking relationships.[4] There are places in its governance for elders, priests, deacons, bishops, teachers—titles similar to those in other schemes of ecclesiastical governance, but with largely different functions. There are also titles such as *prophets* and *apostles*, biblical terms used by Mormons for persons with special roles, but seldom used in the polities of other groups. There are also *wards* and *stakes*—terms for parts of the church structure not found elsewhere. This elaborate panoply of roles, particularly two orders of priesthood, enables the church to involve "all worthy males" in some titular capacity, even though Mormonism essentially is an all-lay movement and does not set any group apart as clergy.[5] Until June 1978, church offices were restricted to white males, but now they are open without regard to race or color.

---

1. *Profiles in Belief: The Religious Bodies of the United States and Canada*, 4 vols. (New York: Harper and Row, 1977–79).

2. Frank S. Mead, *Handbook of Denominations in the United States*, revised by Samuel S. Hill, new 10th ed. (Nashville: Abingdon Press, 1995), 165.

3. Gustav Niebuhr, "Adopting 'Mormon' to Emphasize Christianity," *New York Times*, February 19, 2001.

4. See Kathleen Elgin, *The Church of Jesus Christ of Latter-day Saints*, with a foreword by Ray Kneel (New York: David McKay, 1969), 86. For a detailed description of the organization, emphasizing its hierarchical nature, see the web page http://www.mormons.org/basic/organization/index.htm (consulted May 14, 2001).

5. Thomas F. O'Dea, *The Mormons* (Chicago: University of Chicago Press, 1957), 174.

Priests, Elders, and Bishops

Priesthood among the Mormons functions differently than priesthood in most polities that use that term for ministers. Priesthood in Mormonism is more like eldership—though a special form of eldership, which not only distributes participation widely but which also facilitates, in conjunction with other offices in the church's structure, remarkably effective control of the church from the top. Authority is maintained by enlisting almost every male into some role and giving each a sense of responsibility for what happens in the church. As Thomas O'Dea has suggested, this nullifies clericalism by spreading it widely rather than by abolishing it.[6]

All males who are willing become a part of the system early in their lives. Two lines of priesthood—the Aaronic, or Levitical, priesthood and the higher Melchizedek priesthood—welcome a large percentage of the male members in governance roles starting at an early age. The Aaronic priesthood is composed of young men under twenty; the Melchizedek priesthood consists of those over twenty and often well into their middle years. Entrance to the Aaronic priesthood begins at age twelve with ordination as a *deacon*—a role that assists older officials in the church and involves participation in local meetings called *councils*. The ordination ceremony is not a public laying on of hands but is more like the initiation ceremony into a secret organization, such as the Masons, and involves giving a secret handshake and sharing other secrets that the young priests agree to hold inviolate. After three years, advancement to *teacher* occurs. The role of teacher was originally intended to watch over the deportment of members and the regularity of their participation in church duties. This duty is carried out in cooperation with older men, but it assimilates the junior males to such roles at an early age. They become accustomed to duties that in many other groups would be considered meddling in the personal affairs of others.

After two or three more years, the young man is ordained a *priest* and thus empowered to "preach, teach, expound, exhort,

---

6. For a description of the Mormon organization see ibid., 174–85.

and baptize, and administer the sacrament."[7] Having many priests is considered advantageous by Mormons, since it provides most families with at least one male who can employ consecrated olive oil to aid family members who are sick or troubled. This practice is believed to convey help from God to those in need. The sacramental power of the priests is considered valid only when carried out strictly in accordance with the statutes of the church.

Mormons maintain institutes for the instruction of the young in the faith and duties of the church—instruction that requires a good deal of time and attention and is often offered in special facilities near schools and colleges. Learning about the doctrines and practices of the church is a major aspect of growing up in the church and is taken on by Mormon youth in addition to other learning.

The activities of the Aaronic priesthood occur within the local meeting unit—which in Mormonism is called a *ward* (rather than a parish or congregation). Leadership by young men in worship services comes quickly. Deacons, those between twelve and fourteen, serve the bread and water (not wine!) used in the ordinance of the Lord's Supper, which is celebrated at the weekly meeting. The bread and water have been prepared and blessed for this purpose by slightly older young men who have reached the first level of priesthood. Most prayers used in worship are spontaneous, but a fixed form is used for blessing the bread and water in the Lord's Supper. Sermons or testimonials are delivered by different persons each week, sometimes extemporaneously.[8]

Mormons are expected to attend the ward that covers the geographical area in which they live and not to shop for a more congenial one. Several wards are grouped into *stakes*, which are considerably smaller than a diocese or presbytery and meet quarterly. Mormons do not develop very large wards, since the close support and scrutiny of members that Mormonism exercises would not be feasible in a large gathering.[9] Stakes tend to consist of up

---

7. These words are take from *Doctrine and Covenants*, 20:46. Cited by O'Dea, *Mormons*, 176.

8. See Wallace F. Bennett, *Why I Am a Mormon* (New York: Thomas Nelson and Sons, 1958), 110–11.

9. "Mormon micromanagement extends into all sorts of ward business that other hier-

to a dozen wards. In authority, the stakes are considered primary, the wards derivative.

The term *elder* is used of the first stage of the next order, or Melchizedek priesthood, to which the young man is admitted following service in the three stages of the Aaronic priesthood. The elders meet in a council that can have as many as, but no more than, ninety-six members. The next step in the second order of priesthood is membership in the Seventy. Young men in this order are usually sent on mission—closely supervised work done in pairs at their own expense for eighteen to twenty-four months, either in the United States or overseas. Young women may volunteer for mission assignments of eighteen months. This mission service is looked on as training for more advanced leadership in the church. Elders meet in groups of seventy, presided over by seven presidents, the senior of which exercises the controlling role. The senior level of the Melchizedek priesthood is *high priest*—a rank usually attained at middle age. Many officials of the church are drawn from this group, not only ward leaders and supervisors of the Aaronic priests, but also those in the higher echelons.

The highest office in the ward is that of a *bishop*—a part-time, unpaid administrative and teaching role, assisted by two counselors who are also high priests. Bishops are selected and assigned by a higher authority of the church, called the First Presidency, on the advice of the stake presidency and stake council.

The role of the ward bishop is demanding, even though the bishop has the assistance of the deacons, teachers, and priests of the Aaronic order. The bishop not only controls the affairs of the local ward and conducts services, but supervises the behavior of individual members and their fidelity to church practice. Bishops control the access of Mormons to the temples, in which special ceremonies considered important in determining the eventual (celestial) destiny both of members of the church, and of the relatives and forebears about whose destiny they may assume a vicarious concern, are performed. The Mormon interest in genealogy, which is extensive and remarkably thorough, is carried

---

archical churches leave up to the local clergy and laity. Wards are required to fill out and send in a blizzard of reports" (Richard N. Ostling and Joan K. Ostling, *Mormon America: The Power and the Promise* [San Francisco: HarperSanFrancisco, 1999], 155).

on so Mormons can identify relatives for whose celestial destiny they undergo the temple rituals. Non-Mormons are not allowed inside a temple once it has been set aside for sacred functions, and aspects of the ceremony are secret. The temple ceremonies involve donning special garments and some secret ceremonies.

HIGHER GOVERNANCE ROLES

Higher governance roles in the church will be described by working from the top down rather than from the bottom up. At the top is the president of the church. He is regarded as a prophet, seer, and revealer. The first president is the apostle longest in the service of the church[10]—which means that his selection does not involve a political process. The first president is assisted by two aides whom he appoints, first and second counselors. These three high priests constitute the First Presidency, which has the power to determine the spiritual and temporal direction of the church. The first president is considered able to speak for the Lord in everything. It is believed that his word provides the definitive reading of scripture, that he will never lead the church astray, that he is to be completely trusted. He may make binding judgments about civic and temporal as well as spiritual matters. The power ascribed to the first president in Mormonism is extremely broad. "No spiritual leader of any other sizable denomination, not even the pope of Rome, carries such a status as God's direct spokesman on earth combined with such a thoroughgoing control over a religious organization."[11]

Below the First Presidency stands the Quorum of the Twelve (Apostles), headed by the president of the Twelve. Membership in this group is limited, which means that the principle of widespread participation in the governance of the church has to be modified. The official mode of selection to this role is "by revelation." In practical terms, this means selection by the First Presidency. Admission to the Quorum of the Twelve is achieved by Melchizedek high priests who achieve special visibility—either

---

10. Wallace F. Turner, *The Mormon Establishment* (Boston: Houghton Mifflin, 1966), 3.
11. Ibid., 148.

financial or scholarly—in worldly attainments. Although not political in the sense of involving an elective process, there is an element of covert politics at this point; standing and influence matter.

Below the Quorum of the Twelve is the presidency of the First Quorum of the Seventy. Membership in the Seventy is a step on the rung of the Melchizedek priesthood, just below that of high priest. The term *seventy* is related in part to the size of the groups that meet on this level, under the direction of the Quorum of the Twelve. The Seventies also bring together the young men on mission assignment—their first activity as elders, which, as indicated above, is the first step in the Melchizedek priesthood.

The Aaronic priesthood is supervised by a group of three bishops known as the Presiding Bishopric. This group works under the supervision of the Quorum of the Twelve. The high officials of the church move throughout the church in their supervisory roles. Most of them serve without compensation, other than expenses, and often at considerable expenditure of time and effort.

Faith Practices

Mormonism expects fidelity from its members. The church provides both restrictions on members' behavior and extraordinary support for them in times of need. The tithe is mandatory. Refraining from smoking and the use of alcohol, even from caffeine, is normative. Lifestyles are closely monitored. But persons in need, whether material or spiritual, are promptly aided. The church has built and maintains denominational facilities that are similar in function (not in their architectural design!) to those maintained by Roman Catholicism. These include the headquarters in Salt Lake City—a tourist attraction in and of itself—but also a growing number of elaborate temples around the world. All of this tends to build deep loyalty and makes the church a strong presence in many areas.

The Church of Jesus Christ of Latter-day Saints holds a number of beliefs that are common to other Christian groups, plus special beliefs drawn from the Book of Mormon as well as from a second sacred text called *Doctrine and Covenants*. It is more visible, however, for its practices than for its doctrine. It probably has the most tightly controlled governance of any Christian group— certainly of any Christian group of its size. As a lay movement, it involves young males at an early age and conforms them to its common life with a tenacity that few other groups approach. Obedience to the church is valued more than depth of theological reflection.

The church thus builds a particular character that is zealous in its sense of duty and restraint. It has developed significant cultural institutions, like the Temple Choir of Salt Lake City and the elaborate genealogical libraries it uses for tracing the ancestry of members and graciously shares with the general public. The church has been less successful in developing theologians of note, and it has had difficulty at times maintaining the academic freedom of those who teach in its university.

The church cares for its members' temporal as well as spiritual needs and nurtures them in a supportive community with widespread resources, created by a high level of expected support. The highest officials of the church exercise much control, and the First Presidency is considered to have unquestioned power to discern God's will for the church and its members. The church is essentially a spiritual totalitarianism based on voluntary allegiance and a huge entrepreneurial system professing strong loyalty to American democracy and conventional civic values. It is dynamic, highly disciplined, sacrificially financed, and publicly visible.

Resources for Understanding Mormonism

Bennett, Wallace F. *Why I Am a Mormon.* New York: Thomas Nelson and Sons, 1958.

Bitton, Davis. *Historical Dictionary of Mormonism.* Metuchen, N.J., and London: Scarecrow Press, 1994.

Elgin, Kathleen. *The Mormons: The Church of Jesus Christ of Latter-day Saints.* New York: David McKay, 1969.

Hinkley, Gordon B. *What of the Mormons? Including a Short History of the Church of Jesus Christ of Latter-day Saints.* 6th rev. ed. Salt Lake City: Church of Latter-day Saints, 1954.

Mullen, Robert. *The Latter-day Saints: The Mormons Yesterday and Today.* Garden City, N.Y.: Doubleday, 1966.

O'Dea, Thomas F. *The Mormons.* Chicago: University of Chicago Press, 1957.

Ostling, Richard N., and Joan K. Ostling. *Mormon America: The Power and the Promise.* San Francisco: HarperSanFrancisco, 1999.

Quinn, D. Michael. *The Mormon Hierarchy: Origins of Power.* Salt Lake City: Signature Books, 1994.

Smith, Hyman, and Janet M. Sjodahl, eds. *The Doctrine and Covenants: Containing Revelations Given to Joseph Smith, Jr., the Prophet, with an Introduction and Historical and Exegetical Notes.* Rev. ed. Salt Lake City: Deseret, 1976.

Turner, Wallace. *The Mormon Establishment.* Boston: Houghton Mifflin, 1966.

6

Leadership by Discernment

In Mormonism, as seen in the last chapter, the designation of leadership by appointment and seniority results in a tightly controlled system of governance that delegates authority from the top down and that nourishes conformity and character. The political contests often associated with the elections of church officials are eliminated.

In the broad spectrum of groups associated with the Mennonite heritage and in the Quaker tradition, to which the exposition now turns, leaders have traditionally been selected from the community in a process of discernment. In this process, the decision making (the practice of which varies in form among different groups) is designed to attend to the Spirit. It is more a recognition of gifts and graces than a bestowal of official standing. This also avoids choosing leaders by who can garner the most votes, although people still may register their preferences in discrete and subtle ways.

Mennonite Leadership Values

The values that give the several and quite different Mennonite communities their identity generally include disciplined living and some degree of separation from the world. This makes the Mennonites a "complex socio-religious phenomenon composed of many facets, rather than being only a religious movement."[1] Although Mennonite beliefs are basically similar to those of most Christians, it is not doctrine that identifies the Mennonites as much as their ethical response to the gospel. This response, of

---

1. Calvin Redekop, *Mennonite Society* (Baltimore: Johns Hopkins University Press, 1989), 47.

course, involves convictions, but for Mennonites the term *belief system* "refers to the dynamic nature of the formulations of belief and practice on the part of the Anabaptists as they found themselves set 'over against' the dominant religious and political structures."[2] For many groups in the Anabaptist heritage, Christianity is not merely a matter of churchmanship but of community lifestyle.

Both the sixth section of the Schleitheim Confession of Faith adopted by the Swiss Brethren in 1527, and Article IX of the Dordrecht Confession of Faith adopted by the Dutch Mennonite Conference in 1632, indicate the need for, and place of, spiritual leaders. Both documents stress the exemplifying and teaching functions of such leaders (called "pastors" in the first document, "teachers," "deacons," and "deaconesses" in the second). The wording of these historic documents is sufficiently broad to allow variety in the subsequent branches of Mennonite groups. Some have elders/bishops who support themselves by the same work as others members of the religious family to which they belong; others have ministers especially trained for their task and paid by the congregation so they can devote themselves full-time to their leadership functions. Some groups confine their leadership to males. All, however, expect the leader to exemplify the values of the group. The role of the leaders is facilitative rather than domineering, symbolic and pedagogical rather than sacerdotal. The Anabaptist tradition, out of which the Mennonites came, was strongly anticlerical—yet it did not repudiate the necessity of leadership roles.

GOVERNANCE BY CUSTOM AND TRADITION

The Hutterites are one of the most traditional groups within the Mennonite heritage. Like most Mennonites, they expect that all members will lead lives of special discipline, including refusal of military service and refusal to take oaths. In addition, the Hutterites practice the common ownership of property. There is no line between their existence as a community set apart from the

---

2. Ibid., 48.

world and their existence as an ecclesial community. But this does not relieve them of having to govern themselves; since their total life is affected, it makes their governance even more important than in groups of Christians whose religious life consists only of ecclesiastical involvements.

The Hutterite practice of governance is based on custom and tradition rather than on explicit constitutional law. Its general features, however, reveal a pattern in which human choices are mixed with reliance on the discernment of God's will. The male adults of the local communities make all major decisions, but they elect a council of five or six men who carry on the daily decision making. This council consists of the minister of the colony, a steward (who cares for the property of the community), and two or three other men chosen for these roles for life.

None of these persons is relieved of the obligation to perform the ordinary manual tasks that all members of the Hutterite community perform in order to maintain themselves as an agricultural unit. Those chosen for leadership roles, however, accept the additional duties and seek to fulfill them. Since leadership responsibilities involve extra work and confer no special privileges, it is understandable why the ministerial office is viewed as a responsibility to be accepted rather than a privilege to be sought.

The combination of human choice and reliance on the will of God can be seen in the way in which the minister, or preacher, is chosen. When a community of Hutterites needs a spiritual leader, a service is held in which the brethren of the local community as well as representatives from other communities suggest names of suitable candidates. A presiding elder hears these names and tallies the times they are mentioned. The names of those endorsed five or more times are placed in a hat (or otherwise arranged for a drawing), and the name that comes out becomes the new minister. This person is then ordained by the laying on of hands.[3]

Male members of the community elect the steward and farm manager, but without the involvement of other communities and

---

3. This scenario, which can vary somewhat from group to group, is based on an account in Victor Peters, *All Things Common: The Hutterian Way of Life* (Minneapolis: University of Minnesota Press, 1965), 81.

without the use of the lot. The procedure differs considerably, however, from an open election.

> The medium used is the ballot. There are no nominations and there is no canvassing for votes, as this would lead to expressions of "unbrotherly preferences." Every man puts the name of the man he thinks best qualified for the position on a slip of paper, and the one getting the largest number of votes is declared elected. As colony steward he cannot show any favoritism. If in elections of enterprise heads he should voice a preference for any man the steward could be punished. On the other hand, the colony delegates considerable latitude in decision-making to the steward.[4]

Although the practices of the Hutterites are not followed in all Mennonite groups, they clearly illustrate one of the important aspects of the Mennonite view of leadership. Leadership is designated for service, not to reward victors in a race for the right to exercise power. The choice of leaders is made in a way that discerns the most qualified (or the person that God feels should lead the community) rather than by a process in which candidates campaign to be elected or are chosen by existing authorities seeking to consolidate their influence.

THE PRACTICE OF SHUNNING

Among other Mennonite groups, the Old Order Amish may be closest to the practices of the Hutterites. They worship in private homes, resist cultural change (hence no automobiles), dress plainly, and use the lot as a method of determining who will be their preachers.

One of the distinctive features of Amish practice is the treatment of those whose behavior is considered incompatible with the norms of the group. This takes the forms of shunning, also called avoidance. Since Amish practice involves all of life, exclusion involves more than excommunication from specifically religious activities. According to Article XVII of the Dordrecht Confession, on which this practice is founded, those expelled or censured by the church for perversity of doctrine or wickedness of life are to

---

4. Ibid., 84.

be considered spiritual outcasts. Members in good standing are to have nothing to do with such persons.

To be shunned can be a momentous psychic jolt, particularly in a religious community that provides the context of its members' life. The interesting aspect of this practice is the insistence that it should be healing, not destructive, and hence a certain moderation is associated with its imposition. According to the confession, it is not to be "conducive to the [person's] ruin, but serviceable to the [person's] amendment." The person being shunned is to be fed when hungry (though usually at a different table), visited if sick, not treated as an enemy but exhorted as a brother, and brought back to the proper knowledge of God. The different groups of Mennonites differ in their support of this practice. Some practice it stringently; others doubt its suitability.[5]

CONGREGATIONAL CONFERENCING

Most Mennonite groups view the local congregation, which in many cases is the same as their living community, as the locus of decision making. It decides whom to baptize, whom to admit to membership and on what conditions, who is to conduct worship and to teach, who is to govern, and how much outreach in which it will engage. Congregations also determine how much they will cooperate with other Mennonite congregations. However, considerable conferencing takes place among congregations. Without abandoning their autonomy, Mennonite congregations confer with other congregations within their subgroups about standards of faith, issues of polity and administration, and common mission projects. This conferencing, which has procedural, logistical, and inspirational dimensions, is an important part of Mennonite life—yet it works consultatively and does not function as a superior authority.[6]

Most Mennonite groups that practice separation from the world maintain effective arrangements for mutual aid within their mem-

---

5. See entries under "avoidance" in the index to John C. Wenger, *Glimpses of Mennonite History and Practice* (Scottdale, Pa.: Herald Press, 1949).

6. Redekop, *Mennonite Society*, 62–69.

berships. An example is the "barn raising" in which all neighbors gather and help one of their number in the crucial stage of building, which cannot be done by one or two pair of hands working alone. Those who suffer disasters are aided, as are those in temporal need. The Mennonite Central Committee constitutes an effective organization for coordinating the worldwide charitable and relief work of all groups (some participating somewhat more readily than others). In the opinion of many, the Mennonite Central Committee is an impressive example of Mennonite cooperation and common endeavor.

CHANGES IN POLITY

Not all Mennonite groups have maintained the separation from the world that has marked groups like the Hutterites and the Amish. Several have modified their practices, moving away from decision making by discernment to the acceptance of majority rule.[7] When the Mennonite Church entered negotiations with the General Conference Mennonite Church, they prepared a document specifically addressing a polity for governing ministerial leadership. This document underscores a belief that ministry is performed by all baptized members, but also that there is a place for a special group that includes "pastors, teachers, elders, lay leaders, evangelists, missionaries, pastoral counselors, chaplains, overseers, bishops and church administrators."[8]

A historical section in this document recounts the changes in the polity of the Anabaptist and Mennonite churches since the sixteenth century. According to this section, although there have been different forms, a functional threefold ministry developed that included elders/bishops, preachers, and deacons. The lot was in common use for choosing ministers until the middle of the twentieth century. Bishops exercised sacramental functions within congregations or groups of congregations over which they had oversight; deacons were in charge of the congregations' alms

---

7. *A Mennonite Polity for Ministerial Leadership*, ed. Everett J. Thomas (Newton, Kans.: Faith and Life Press, 1996), 5.
8. Ibid., 18f.

funds. This threefold "bench" (as it was called in Mennonite circles) was fairly typical by the middle of the twentieth century, but it would soon give way to further changes. The supervisory role of bishops was undercut by a growing suspicion of centralized authority that developed at the time, and the deacons' benevolence role became less clear as the need for service to the poor diminished. This brought about a change in practice.

> In the search for a new organizational model the terminology of the office changed from *deacon* to *elder*, and these persons were normally selected for three-year time periods. In the process of change the minister took on a more central role in the congregations with support from the elders group. In other cases, administration of the congregation fell increasingly to a church council comprised of members elected or placed in position through a gifts discernment process. In some cases the church council began to view itself as a "board of directors" for the congregation with the pastor serving as their "employee."[9]

Mennonite polity in groups that have adapted to life in the ordinary world has come to be an example of the associational congregationalism that will be discussed in chapter 8. Associations have developed to give special attention to the "credentialing" of ministers. The selection and training of those who devote full-time service in a ministerial office, and the call process by which congregations find ministers, are now coordinated through a department of ministerial leadership. Conference ministers (sometimes also called bishops) serve as executives in these matters. The polity for ministerial leadership developed jointly by the Mennonite Church and the General Conference Mennonites has facilitated the placing of ministers in positions open in either group. Congregations continue to have final authority concerning who will lead them, but the associations' work greatly aids them in finding the most fitting candidates and in providing criteria by which the educational and spiritual level of ministerial leadership is credentialed.

---

9. Ibid., 45.

Discerning the Spirit
within the Society of Friends

For Quakers, governance is more a matter of discerning the Spirit than of creating institutional structures or exercising official roles. Quakers have contributed much to the improvement of society at large, not because they offer a model for democratic government that deals with power through political means (as did various churches in the Reformed tradition), but because their noteworthy adherence to principles of compassion and nonviolence has served to make the world, wherever their influence has permeated, more humane. Quakers belong to that family of Christian groups that expects highly visible allegiance to a way of life rooted in the New Testament—a way to be followed by each person and not merely by a dedicated minority of clergy or members of religious orders set apart for special achievement.

Sometimes it is suggested that the Society of Friends tries to live without ecclesiastical governance. The Quakers have no paid clergy; they do not take votes in order to make decisions; they eschew formally designated rankings that carry unique authority; and they rely for support on generosity stemming from devotion rather than on assessments imposed by fiat.

> For 300 years Friends have sat in outward silence as each person would pray, meditate, or "listen to the Light of God" within himself or herself and within the group. Until recently, their only "ministry" rose out of such "listening," when any member of the group felt led inwardly to offer a specific message, prayer, or song. Individuals who "appeared in ministry" often and helpfully were faithfully "recorded" and invited to sit on the "facing bench" at the front of the meeting house, along with the men or women "Elders" who provided guidance and counsel for the Meeting community.[10]

Elders in the Quaker tradition—whether called by that name or not—guide and counsel the gathering of Friends. They do this by virtue of their spiritual qualities, their exemplification of Quaker characteristics, their maturity and depth of character. Members of

---

10. Hugh Barbour and J. William Frost, *The Quakers* (New York and Westport, Conn.: Greenwood Press, 1988), 4.

the meeting do not need to vote for elders to have power; elders already lead by stature. According to Elton Trueblood, this process did not do away with ministers, but provided an alternative way of discerning them. "The thoughtful reader is likely to wonder how anyone knew who a Quaker minister was, since there was nothing in the nature of an ordination ceremony. The answer is that Friends watched in order to see. A minister was simply one who ministered. If a man or woman began to speak well and effectively, everyone knew it and that was the end of the matter."[11]

Quakers organize under the rubric of "meetings." They do not use the terms *congregations* or *presbyteries, wards* or *stakes, conferences* or *conventions*. But the structure of Quaker governance is not that different (except in terminology) from that of many other Christian groups. It moves from local to regional and to larger regional meetings.

> The monthly meeting is the basic unit, made up of one or more meetings (groups) in a neighborhood. It convenes each week for worship and once a month for business. It keeps records of membership, births, deaths, and marriages, appoints committees, considers queries on spiritual welfare, and transacts all business. Monthly meetings join four times a year in a quarterly meeting to stimulate spiritual life and decide on any business that should be brought to the attention of the yearly meeting. The yearly meeting corresponds to a diocese in an episcopal system. There are 27 in the U.S. and Canada, in touch with Friends all over the world. There are standing committees on such subjects as publications, education, the social order, missions, peace, charities, and national legislation; trust fund incomes are allocated, and the work of the society is generally supervised.[12]

Quaker procedure, however, does differ significantly from most other governance. Quakers deliberate according to the Spirit rather than according to parliamentary rules. They seek "the sense of the meeting" rather than a majority vote. If they are divided, they may meditate further until a common mind emerges; they

---

11. D. Elton Trueblood, *The People Called Quakers* (New York: Harper and Row, 1966), 110.

12. Frank S. Mead and Samuel S. Hill, *Handbook of Denominations in the United States*, new 10th ed. (Nashville: Abingdon Press, 1995), 146.

may postpone an action; or they may assign a problem to committee for further study. Minority opinion is won over, not voted down. On the local level, business is done with full participation—including women as well as men. The larger bodies are composed of delegates, but once assembled they deliberate as a cohesive whole. Because Quakers will not take action if there is continuing opposition, considered from the perspective of other groups Quaker practice seems to give veto power to the minority; looked at from the Quaker perspective, the practice assures that governance empowers the community rather than divides it.

LIVING A DISCIPLINED LIFE

Throughout much of its history, the Society of Friends has been concerned that its members live a disciplined life. To this end, Quakers drew up documents indicating the conduct expected of its members—documents that indicate both expected standards of behavior and that record actions taken against those whose conduct was considered inappropriate. Queries were employed in meetings to prompt examination of members' behavior, and overseers were appointed to enforce rules fairly and consistently. Infractions could lead to a request for public apology and even to "disownment."

> If the offense were serious—marriage by a priest or to a non-Quaker, drunkenness, fighting, fornication—the matter came directly to the Monthly Meeting. The Women's Meeting investigated all charges relating to women; the men's for men. Usually the Meeting selected a committee to visit the person. If he or she admitted a mistake, the committee required an acknowledgement in writing that the Meeting accepted, judging the sincerity of penitence by his or her sorrow for past transgression and future good behavior. If the written apology were not explicit or contrite enough, the meeting might require amplification.
>
> If the offender refused to change his or her ways or to acknowledge errors, the Meeting could make one last try to reclaim the person, or it could proceed at once to disownment.[13]

---

13. Barbour and Frost, *Quakers*, 110.

Church discipline was not unknown in other churches at the time it was widely practiced by the Quakers, but Quakers gave it special features. Not only did they discipline those who married outside the group or who committed serious breaches of moral norms, they came to disown (not without controversy) those who owned slaves. They advocated simplicity (but not uniqueness) in dress and a "becoming sobriety" in manners. Interestingly, despite the pacifism in their tradition, they did not make willingness to perform military service a cause for discipline. Moreover, Quaker practice has provided not only scrutiny of unacceptable behavior but guidance for members in making important decisions. Such guidance is offered by a "clearness committee" that, when requested, convenes to help a member make an important decision.[14]

Although discipline of personal misbehavior has tended to decrease over the years (as it has in most Christian groups), the Quakers' concern for society has grown into one of their most impressive features. Quakers have been in the forefront of movements for social reform and distinguished for their work in alleviating human suffering. The American Friends Service Committee, formed in 1917 to provide an opportunity for Quakers who objected to service in the armed forces to serve their country, has subsequently become one of the most respected privately operated relief and service agencies in the world. The Quakers have also founded some of the most impressive educational institutions in the United States.

In both the various Mennonite groups and in the Quaker tradition, the congregation (or local meeting) has played a more important role in shaping church life than in any of the polities previously described. Although they rely on nonpolitical means for designating leadership, the practices of these groups also suggest another governance model, that of congregational governance. Although, in the Quaker tradition, congregations are governed by the Spirit, law and politics become operative in other forms

---

14. For an account of how such committees work, see Parker J. Palmer, *The Courage to Teach: Exploring the Inner Landscape of a Teacher's Life* (San Francisco: Jossey-Bass, 1998), 152f. One could fairly call this process lay pastoral counseling by discernment.

of congregationalism. The next section examines several ways in which this process occurs.

Resources on Leadership by Discernment

For Understanding the Mennonite Family of Traditions

Hostetler, John A. *Amish Society.* 4th ed. Baltimore and London: Johns Hopkins University Press, 1993.

Peters, Victor. *All Things Common: The Hutterian Way of Life.* Minneapolis: University of Minnesota Press, 1965.

Redekop, Calvin. *Mennonite Society.* Baltimore: Johns Hopkins University Press, 1989.

Thomas, Everett J., ed. *A Mennonite Polity for Ministerial Leadership.* Newton, Kans.: Faith and Life Press, 1996.

Wenger, John C. *Glimpses of Mennonite History and Practice.* Scottdale, Pa.: Herald Press, 1949.

For Understanding the Society of Friends

Barbour, Hugh, and J. William Frost. *The Quakers.* New York and Westport, Conn.: Greenwood Press, 1988.

Elgin, Kathleen. *The Quakers: The Religious Society of Friends.* New York: David McKay, 1968.

Trueblood, D. Elton. *The People Called Quakers.* New York: Harper and Row, 1966.

Part Three

GOVERNANCE BY CONGREGATIONS

7

CONNECTIVE
CONGREGATIONALISM

THE THIRD MAJOR TYPE of church governance locates the essence of the church within the local association of believers, who endeavor to live in response to the gospel according to their convictions as to its meanings and its demands. As with the other types of church governance, this congregational pattern comes in several variations.

Some of the most conservative and some of the most liberal theological stances are found in groups with a congregational form of governance. Similarly, some congregationally organized denominations are liturgical; others—possibly the majority—are put off by formality in worship. Some denominations are characterized by ethnic identifications or ethnic origins, others by geographical influences. Some of these differences characterize the denominations themselves—or large clusters of churches within the denomination—but other contrasts may appear among individual churches within the same denomination. Although individual congregations have the advantage of involving people directly in determining how the Christian community lives, judgments as to normative Christian belief and proper practice are apt to vary considerably when made by local communities of faith.

One of the most cherished aspects of congregational polities is the freedom they offer—a freedom that varies in extent from one form of congregationalism to the next—for people to find their own ways of achieving Christian authenticity in association with their immediate associates and with congregations of similar persuasion. This freedom is exercised in professed obedience to the gospel as understood by the local body of believers.

In most congregational polities, the local church is not dependent on the power or standing of a hierarchy or a collegium to guide its beliefs or to legitimize its sacramental observances. It lives its discipleship by its own reading of the gospel and by the measures it develops for determining when that reading is faithful and legitimate. There are congregational polities, however, in which local congregations cooperate with each other in order to create a distinctive group identity, whether as to belief or practice. In such polities, there is a strong connectional interest in determining what constitutes proper and legitimate faith and practice.

This chapter will examine such connective congregationalism. In this pattern, local churches come together because they believe that only insofar as there is widespread agreement as to the nature of Christian faith and practice can claims for "catholicity" be sustained. In connectional congregationalism, churches have some supervisory interaction with each other. While the authority in this model remains in the local parish, that authority is exercised in connection with, and to some extent over, that of other congregations. There is an effort to obtain commonality in faith and practice that provides distinguishing features to the ecclesial family. Creeds are usually involved and considered important. Patterns of worship may also be similar. Acceptance of such standards comes about, however, because they are adopted by the congregations acting together and not because they are imposed by a supervisory "over-body" with an existence prior to, or an authority superior to, that of the local congregations.

Chapter 8 will examine associational congregationalism. In this pattern, local churches are freer to shape their practices according to their own judgment about the gospel's requirements. But they cooperate with one another for support and reinforcement. To be sure, any form of cooperation presupposes some judgment as to the suitability of individual churches to be members of a larger association. But in associational congregationalism, control over individual parishes is far less decisive than in connective congregationalism. When normative statements of belief or general rules of practice are developed, local congregations may give them respectful attention, but they are not mandated to adopt them.

The third major alternative is a congregationalism which has no overstructures. One form congregationalism takes is theological objection to forming a denomination. The other form is complete local independence, in which individual churches pursue their own agendas with little or no accountability to wider groups. I discuss congregational polities of this pattern in chapter 9.

LUTHERAN GOVERNANCE

It may be that no mainline or major denomination is characterized by a completely operative connectional congregationalism—after all, the idea embodies a dialectical contrast between two principles: local determination and denominational control. Nevertheless, a number of Lutheran groups have developed polities that provide connections among congregations that result in significant uniformity of beliefs and practice.

Lutherans provide a fascinating group for the study of polity. They differ significantly from most church bodies in that their polity has taken different forms and directions depending on times and circumstance. Lutheran polities not infrequently have developed in response to historical and contingent circumstances rather than from deliberate and theoretical design. There is nothing about the designation *Lutheran* that carries a meaning similar to that of the terms *Episcopal, Presbyterian,* or *Congregational.* Lutherans have frequently had bishops whose governing functions (though not their sacerdotal roles) have made Lutheran polity akin to a clearly defined episcopal polity. This is especially true of many European Lutherans.

At other times, Lutherans have developed governance patterns roughly analogous to those of presbyterianism—although without an ordained group of lay elders and lacking a carefully guarded parity between clergy and laity above the parish level. At still other times, Lutherans have embraced a congregational means of conducting ecclesiastical affairs. While these developments have made for interesting and varied patterns in Lutheran polity, they have also required Lutheranism to deal with the problems of having a plurality of procedures within the same ecclesiastical family. Lutherans are probably more apt to be discussing polity among themselves than vigorously defending a particular form of polity as an essential mark of the church.

The variation in Lutheran ecclesiology is not without its reason for being. When Lutheranism first emerged, governance of the church was exercised largely by princes, who governed the secular affairs of the territories. There was little pressure to devise a clear and binding polity by which the church could conduct its own affairs. Theologically speaking, the governance of the church was treated as a matter of secondary importance—something of human making and not of divine instigation. The decisive mark of the church was located in faithfulness to God's word as measured by doctrine and sacraments—not by polity. Lutherans observed, possibly with warrant, that no one form of church governance can be determined from the New Testament—although the New Testament does commend the formation of churches as institutions. Luther himself provided no definitive suggestions for the organization of church life. The result has been aptly characterized by a Lutheran scholar as follows:

> Lutherans historically regarded forms not as right or wrong but as helpful or unhelpful. No form is at the *esse* of the church. The only possible exception to this generalization is that an office of the ministry is *de jure divino* (by divine command) but even this office is functional and, while necessary, may be argued for in a variety of ways. Without forms no Gospel can be proclaimed, no sacraments administered, and the life of no Christian community can be structured. At the same time, the most that can be said for any particular form is that it may be in a given historical-sociological situation for the *bene esse* (well being) of the faith community. It is therefore not accidental that there has never developed anything analogous to a commonly accepted canon law within the Lutheran tradition. Unfortunately there has been little substantive wrestling with questions of form and polity, partly because such matters came to be regarded as adiaphora and partly because of a naiveté regarding church leadership.[1]

---

1. Leigh D. Jordahl, "American Lutheranism: Ethos, Style, and Polity," in *The Lutheran Church in North American Life*, ed. John E. Groh and Robert H. Smith (St. Louis: Clayton, 1979), 35.

When Lutherans came to the United States, there was nothing in their view of church governance preventing them from modifying ecclesiastical procedures to take advantage of the freedom afforded religious groups in a country without a state church. Indeed, the lack of political-church structures in this new context required that new structures of ecclesiastical governance be devised. Although bishops were common in Europe—especially in Swedish Lutheranism—they were not seen as sacerdotally necessary, even though the Swedish Lutherans did maintain an unbroken line of apostolic succession. Bishops were thus not considered—at least by many—as necessary for the church in the new colonies. Much colonial Lutheranism consequently developed essentially congregational forms of governance, providing the members of local churches considerable choice in conducting their affairs. Pastors, elders, and deacons were chosen by the people and performed their respective roles as directed (or subject to review) by the congregation's communicant members (in those days, the males).

The resulting independence was not without problems. Congregations developed different patterns of governance. At times they complained about their ministers. Sometimes such complaints were dealt with by appeal to church authorities in Europe, but other times the complaints drew attention among several churches and the ministers in neighboring areas. This led to the creation of interparochial associations.

THE DEVELOPMENT OF SYNODS

Differences among Lutherans from different parts of Europe as well as among Lutherans in different sections of the colonies made cooperation difficult, but by the eve of the American Revolution, regional associations—variously called synods, presbyteries, united congregations, collegium pastori, ministerii, united preachers, consistories, coeti—were meeting regularly and dealing with church affairs.

Both lay and ministerial representatives from local congregations participated in the regional groups, although the examination of candidates for ordination was reserved for the ministers,

as were doctrinal matters. Such groups, however, did not constitute the locus, as in presbyterian polity, from which the authority
of the church stemmed. Churches could be created without the
groups' explicit permission. Parishes derived their being from the
people that banded to form them rather than from a body with
the exclusive power to establish and supervise local Christian
communities.

Cooperating groups were formed in several regions in the last
quarter of the eighteenth century and the first quarter of the
nineteenth century. A plan to unite these groups into a General
Synod was drafted in 1819 and put into effect two years later.
The move to have a central organization did not have universal
support, "but in time the advantages of Lutheran union prevailed
over such misgivings and by the middle of the nineteenth century most Lutheran Synods in the Eastern states were connected
with the General Synod." The General Synod, however, was an
association of groups that retained most of their former rights and
powers rather than a central authority that preempted them.[2]

THE MISSOURI SYNOD

The congregational aspect of Lutheranism can be seen clearly in
the ecclesiastical practices of an important Lutheran group known
as the Missouri Synod. The Missouri Synod was formed by a group
of Lutherans who emigrated from Saxony in 1838, and who joined
with Lutherans sharing their doctrinal conservatism in Ohio and
in neighboring states. They were led by Rev. Martin Stephan and
other ministers. Upon arrival in the United States, the group made
Stephan its bishop, and other ministers were enjoined to be obe-
dient to his leadership. But before too long Stephan became rigid
and autocratic (some accounts say despotic); he was deposed in
what was essentially a revolt.

The group's polity was consequently altered under the leadership of Rev. C. F. W. Walther and a constitution drawn up that

---

2. This account and the quoted material are drawn from Theodore G. Tappert, "Lutheran Ecclesiastical Government in the United States of America," in *Episcopacy in the
Lutheran Church: Studies in the Development and Definition of the Office of Church Leadership*,
ed. Ivar Asheim and Victor R. Gold (Philadelphia: Fortress Press, 1970), 156–65.

provided for congregational elections of pastors, elders, and deacons. They would exercise sovereign control over the spiritual and temporal affairs of their parishes, under the advisory surveillance of the larger group called the synod. The local control provided the congregationalism; the synod provided the connectionalism. This unique, somewhat paradoxical juxtaposition of two principles has provided the context for bitter struggles in the Missouri Synod's recent history.

The Missouri Synod has not been known for its theological openness; to the contrary, it has been a staunch defender of a particular type of theological orthodoxy and often of exclusionary practices (such as closed communion) that have tended to isolate it from other branches of Christendom—even from other branches of Lutheranism. Many of the issues within its corporate life have revolved around the defense of that orthodoxy. But that defense has not come from a hierarchical authority acting in a monarchical manner. Rather, the defense has resulted from a political process working through the synodical structure. Congregations send delegates to meetings of the Synod, which elects its own officers. The chief officer of the Synod was long designated as president (not bishop). Election of the president can turn into a highly political process, and groups favoring particular agendas often form in order to line up votes. These struggles have sometimes resembled power politics more than clerical hegemony.[3]

Unlike the office of the moderator in presbyterian polity, the office of synodical president involves supervisory powers. If the president has been elected on a platform—to be rigorous in the defense of orthodoxy, for instance—the president is likely to pursue that agenda with determination. This happened in 1969 in the Missouri Synod, when its conservative wing elected a president determined to increase conformity to a strongly conservative theological stance. Many Lutherans have been deeply disturbed and sharply critical of the manner in which the synodical leader has exercised power.

---

3. See F. Dean Lueking, *Grace under Pressure: One Congregation's Testimony* (Richmond: Skipworth Press, 1979), chap. 3, esp. 73.

The first target of presidential action was the Synod bureau-cracy. The president identified staff members not considered sufficiently orthodox and relieved them of their duties. The next targets were the institutions supported by the Synod, such as schools and seminaries. There is a clear synodical authority over such institutions and those who work in them. Synodical mis-sionary activity was likewise scrutinized for conformity to the denomination's agenda. Those who worked in any of these con-texts were subject to adverse action, because their work was a direct function of the Synod. The ax fell most heavily on clergy members who worked in these special contexts, since they were expected to be examples of orthodox belief and proper practice, but the changes also affected laypersons employed by the affected boards or institutions.

When events like this occur pressures can also build on con-gregations, but since the basic polity is congregational they are not as vulnerable as the central bureaucracy or church-supported institutions. But they are not unaffected. They may seek to al-ter the president's policy, but they are not likely to be heeded. They can offer spiritual and temporal support to those adversely affected by synodical actions, but they cannot cancel action taken against such persons by Synod officials. Locally, they can continue to offer parish life that differs from what Synod officers seek, but they may be criticized for doing so. As a last resort, they can vote to withdraw from the Synod, but doing so makes their Lu-theran identity problematic. None of these modes of resistance is undertaken lightly, nor does the fact that a congregation need not knuckle under to the Synod agenda make it easier to deal with situations in which the local congregation is not supportive of a particular synodical stance.

Connectional Aspects of Lutheran Polity

The connectional aspect of Lutheran congregationalism has con-sequences that cannot be easily ignored or lightly dismissed.[4]

---

4. For an account of one congregation under theological siege from the Synod, see ibid.

While theoretically free to determine their own sense of what it means to be a Christian community, local congregations cannot ignore the oversight of a body seen as a means of guiding proper practice and insuring correct doctrine. Individual churches usually cherish their membership in the Synod, find support and authentication, and most commonly take an active interest in what is done on the corporate level. While local parishes in this governance pattern are churches in their own right, not by virtue of their membership in a corporate body, they are expected to be places where the gospel is preached authentically and where the sacraments are administered properly. The policies of the Synod tend to become the standards against which the local congregation is judged as to whether these standards are being observed.

There is a tension between the congregational premise and the expectation that the churches will rightly preach the word and correctly administer the sacraments.

> The congregationalism expressed in the repeated assertion that the Synod was only an advisory body was outweighed by the actual supervisory powers of the president, by the exemption of matters of doctrine and conscience from lay vote, and by the veneration of the clergy (and especially of prominent clergymen), which remained a Missouri characteristic. Synodical authority increased in fact if not in name when the Missouri Synod grew by leaps and bounds and it became necessary to divide the territory of the Synod into districts.[5]

These developments took place, not merely because the Synod was expected to exercise supervisory authority, but also because authority over some key matters was vested largely in the Synod's clergy. Lutherans in general are at home with a high view of the ministry—viewing it as an office ordered by divine intention, but not necessarily dependent on ordination by a higher order of clergy (bishops). In fact, individual Lutheran congregations have at times performed ordinations of pastors, although having wider bodies involved in the examination and ordination

---

5. Tappert, "Lutheran Ecclesiastical Government," 169.

of candidates has become all but a universal practice and has both added to the status of the clergy and to the supervisory clout of the Synod.

Although Lutherans have often had bishops, who have exercised administrative and coordinating functions, they have not been considered alone to possess the power to ordain pastors. Even today, when considerable liturgical uniformity has developed in much Lutheran life and increasing importance has been attached to bishops, they are not set apart from other clergy in any sacerdotal sense. For instance, their vestments are the same as those of regular pastors. But among Protestants, second only perhaps to Episcopalians, Lutheran clergy are the group who most often wear attire that distinguishes them from the laity. Attire is a clue that Lutherans have a high view of the ministry and a polity in which there is only one order (or level) of ministry.

Lutheranism also tends to conduct worship according to a prescribed order that is fairly similar from parish to parish. This does not make liturgy a unifying aspect to the extent that the *Book of Common Prayer* provides the basis for Episcopal identity, but it nevertheless is a significant aspect of Lutheran ecclesiology.

THE EVANGELICAL LUTHERAN CHURCH
IN AMERICA

While the congregationalism of the Missouri Synod is more conspicuous than the congregational element in most other branches of American Lutheranism, all Lutheranism stresses the primacy of the local parish. The congregational element is also evident, though less clearly, in the larger Evangelical Lutheran Church in America.

This Lutheran body was formed in 1988 by the merger of the Lutheran Church in America, the American Lutheran Church, and the Association of Evangelical Lutheran Churches—the latter having broken in 1976 from the Lutheran Church–Missouri Synod. The administrative and coordinating officers of the ELCA are called "bishops," but they are not regarded as carrying historical continuity from which the validity of the church's ministry is bestowed. The constitution and bylaws declare "The Church is a people created by God in Christ, empowered by the Holy Spirit and sent to bear witness to God's creative, redeeming, and sanctifying activity in the world." Behind this statement lies a polity in which individual churches work together in sixty-four geographical synods and one non-geographical synod on a wide variety of common tasks.[6] These groups select leaders to facilitate this cooperation.

Each synod is served by a *bishop*, elected for one term rather than for life, whose role is that of preacher, teacher, and administrator of the sacraments, but also that of president and executive officer. Committed to the concept of a single order (or level) of ministerial office—centered in proclaiming the word of God and administering the holy sacraments—the ministry of the church "embraces both the ministry of the pastor within and for the local community of believers, and of bishop within and for the communion of local communities."[7]

The responsibilities of the bishops are set forth in seven areas: worship and spiritual oversight; pastoral care; mission planning; mission interpretation; mission administration; ecumenical relations; and liaison (among various organizations, agencies, and institutions of the church).[8] Bishops in the ELCA have a well-defined role in the call system by which Lutheran congregations find their pastors, and the protocol is carefully drawn to insure that the process will be orderly. This arrangement gives the bishops significant influence in the process but does not, strictly speaking, abrogate the power of the local congregation to determine its pastor.

The Evangelical Lutheran Church is elaborately organized on the churchwide level. There is a *presiding bishop*, who like the synodical bishops combines the preaching, teaching, and sacramental roles with those of a chief executive officer. The presiding bishop

---

6. *Anatomy of the Evangelical Lutheran Church in America.* http://www.elca.org/co/anatomy.html (consulted October 15, 2000).

7. This wording appears in the preamble to the *Relational Agreement among Synodical Bishops of the Evangelical Lutheran Church in America* in a section significantly entitled, "The Office of the Bishop within the Office of Ministry." Taken from http://www.elca.org/ea/cleo/relationalagreement.html (consulted October 15, 2000).

8. Ibid.

serves a six-year term. He or she chairs a biennial Churchwide Assembly and the Church Council and is assisted by a vice-president, a layperson who serves without salary and who can preside if the presiding bishop is unable to do so. The Church Council meets twice a year "to hear reports, deliberate, set direction and carry on the churchwide organization as the interim legislative authority between the meetings of the Churchwide Assembly."[9] A Conference of Bishops brings together the sixty-five synodical bishops at least twice a year for spiritual renewal and theological enrichment and to make decisions about cooperation—particularly in the call system.

Another clue that points to the congregational premises of Lutheranism is the practice of confirming new members, done by the pastor of the local congregation. While bishops are concerned with individual parishes as well as the larger church organization, and may visit parishes in order to express concern about their welfare, that concern is generally more pastoral than controlling. In this respect, Lutheran bishops are similar to Episcopal bishops, even though their liturgical functions are less crucial. The tension that marked discussions between the ELCA and the Episcopal Church regarding mutual recognition of ministers concerned whether a bishop in the historic continuity is needed to ordain clergy.

Despite the minor variations in history and polity, Timothy Lull, in a judgment that can apply to Lutherans in general, writes: "The strength of the Lutheran church continues to be at the parish level.... Most [Lutherans] have felt the congregations to be the primary reality, and the wider church a secondary and more problematic matter."[10] But, as Lull explains, assuring validity for the word and sacraments requires connections among congregations in order to guard against idiosyncratic manifestations of local control, or a parish life that bears little resemblance to practices of the wider church.

---

9. *Anatomy of the Lutheran Church.*

10. Timothy F. Lull, "The Catholicity of the Local Congregation," in *The New Church Debate: Issues Facing American Lutheranism*, ed. Carl E. Braaten (Philadelphia: Fortress Press, 1983), 140.

Lull shares a growing feeling among Lutherans that there is an indispensable place for bishops in Lutheran polity. These Lutherans differ in the way they define the role of the bishop, but, as Lull suggests, referring to efforts to bring unity among different branches of Lutheranism,

> We are likely to have bishops of some sort in a future Lutheran church. There are plenty of proposals being made about what it is that bishops now do that is essential and what it is that they ought to be doing in a new church. Some see bishops as administrators, and there is much present reality to that. Some hope for bishops who are theologians. Some hope for bishops who will be pastors to pastors. The demands of modern bureaucracy are likely to ensure that whatever bishops do they will spend most of their time in meetings.[11]

COOPERATIVE RELATIONS AND ECCLESIOLOGY

The negotiations concerning how Lutherans can cooperate with other Christian denominations are particularly revealing about Lutheran ecclesiology. The historical legacy that has made governance of secondary significance for Lutherans provides a freedom to consider changing Lutheran polity (or for treating it casually) in ways that would be difficult, if not impossible, for denominations with carefully defined and theologically pivotal forms of governance. There is, however, a paradoxical feature to this freedom. How can Lutherans relate to Christian bodies in which a particular polity is viewed as an essential mark of the church? Can Lutherans, for instance, argue (as some do) for the importance of a historical episcopacy, yet maintain that it is primarily facilitative rather than definitive? Lutheran efforts to develop cooperation with Episcopalians faced disagreement on this issue; it created considerable discussion in Lutheran circles and even held up the agreement's consummation for some time. Can Lutherans who advocate acceptance of the historic episcopacy as normally understood—in contrast to Lutherans who consider bishops useful administratively but not mandated theologically—avoid contra-

---

11. Ibid., 148f.

dicting the premise that matters of governance cannot be made essential to defining the church?[12]

Similar problems might also arise from efforts to relate Lutherans to bodies in the Reformed tradition that regard representative governance by ordained elders as essential to being faithful to the Bible and to the Christian heritage. For Lutherans both bishops and elders can be accepted as matters of indifference, but this is not the case with respect to bishops for many Episcopalians or with respect to elders for some in the Reformed tradition. That such issues have not arisen as strongly with respect to the Lutheran concordat with the churches of the Reformed tradition as they have with respect to the agreement with the Episcopalians suggests that feelings about bishops run stronger than feelings about elders. The Lutheran position has enabled it to work out agreements with churches with two very different forms of governance. Their achievement suggests it is possible to achieve cooperation without necessarily having complete agreement on the fundamentals of polity. That is a position Lutherans have lived with for a long time, and it has positioned them uniquely in contemporary efforts at ecumenical cooperation.

RESOURCES FOR UNDERSTANDING LUTHERANISM

Asheim, Ivar, and Victor R. Gold, eds. *Episcopacy in the Lutheran Church: Studies in the Development and Definition of the Office of Church Leadership.* Philadelphia: Fortress Press, 1970.

Braaten, Carl E., ed. *The New Church Debate: Issues Facing American Lutheranism.* Philadelphia: Fortress Press, 1983.

Formula of Agreement between the Evangelical Lutheran Church in America, the Presbyterian Church (U.S.A.), the Reformed Church in America, and the United Church of Christ: On Entering into Full Communion on the Basis of a Common Calling. http://www.elca.org/Relationships/presbyterian/formula.html.

Groh, John E., and Robert H. Smith, eds. *The Lutheran Church in North America.* St. Louis: Clayton, 1979.

---

12. For treatment of these matters, see Daniel F. Martensen, ed., *Concordat of Agreement: Supporting Essays* (Minneapolis: Augsburg Press, 1995).

Lueking, F. Dean. *Grace under Pressure: One Congregation's Testimony.* Richmond: Skipworth Press, 1979.

Martensen, Daniel F., ed. *Concordat of Agreement: Supporting Essays.* Minneapolis: Augsburg Press, 1995.

Nelson, E. Clifford, in collaboration with Theodore G. Tappert. *The Lutherans in North America.* Rev. ed. Philadelphia: Fortress Press, 1980.

Wolf, Richard C. *Documents of Lutheran Unity in America.* Philadelphia: Fortress Press, 1966.

8

ASSOCIATIONAL CONGREGATIONALISM

PROVISIONS FOR ECCLESIAL CONTROL are present in different forms and to various degrees in each of the polities described in the previous chapters. This control may be said to operate either from the top down or from the sides in, but, in any case, the local parish is subject to requirements or expectations that come from its denomination. Procedures for monitoring local congregations are provided explicitly in polities with bishops and in polities with presbyteries (or their counterparts). Forms of control also develop with less explicit provisions in connectional congregationalism, in which churches monitor each other in ways that create considerable pressures for allegiance to what constitutes that denomination's understanding of the gospel.

THE FREE CHURCH TRADITION

We now come to polities in which freedom is given greater emphasis than control. Such freedom is reserved for the local congregation, so that members may follow their consciences in working out their own ways of being faithful to the gospel. Denominations of such polity come in a number of variations but together are commonly described as "churches in the free church tradition." Although these churches differ in the ways they work out faithfulness, they are similar in locating ecclesial authority within the community of believers. We might, therefore, say that authority comes from the bottom up in their polities.

The term *independency* has sometimes been used to describe the free church tradition—often in a polemical way. For instance, a Presbyterian, writing in the early nineteenth century when church polity was a source of much controversy, made this unsympathetic comment:

> Independents and Congregationalists commit the whole govern-
> ment and discipline of their churches immediately to the body of
> the communicants. In some of their churches all the communi-
> cants, male and female, have an equal voice. In others, the males
> only take part in discipline. In the estimation of Presbyterians this
> mode of conducting ecclesiastical discipline is liable to most seri-
> ous objection. They consider it wholly unsupported by Scripture;
> as "setting those to judge, in many cases, who are least esteemed
> in the church"; as extremely unfavorable to the calm and wise
> administration of justice; nay, as of all the forms of ecclesiastical
> discipline, most exposed to the sway of ignorance, prejudice, pas-
> sion, and artful intrigue; that, under the guise of liberty, it often
> leads to the most grievous tyranny; and is adapted to exert an
> injurious influence on the character both of the pastor and the
> people.[1]

For Independents, on the other hand, the freedom of the local community has been devoutly espoused, not only as most consistent with the practice of the early Christians and hence more biblical than alternatives, but as a view that fosters the regeneration of life among all members.

Independents have argued that other polities either encourage or allow a special class to carry the burden of being Christian and tend to create a laity that is lax or callous in living according to Christian standards. Although the kind of polemic against the free church tradition cited above would likely not be written today, it indicates the extent to which congregational polities reverse assumptions about the most functional ways of maintaining the purity and vitality of the churches. In congregational polity, the vitality of the church is held to depend on a firm foundation of zealous fidelity within a local community of truly committed believers.

This emphasis on the regenerated life of all members of the believing community is crucial to understanding the origins of free

---

1. Samuel Miller, "Presbyterianism: The Truly and Primitive Apostolical Constitution of the Church of Christ," reprinted in David W. Hall and Joseph H. Hall, eds., *Paradigms in Polity* (Grand Rapids, Mich.: Eerdmans, 1994), 98.

church polities. James H. Rigg, whose advocacy of free church polity was influential in the late nineteenth century, citing an important treatise of the time wrote:

> The leading principles of Congregational Independency are three, of which, however, the first is not always taken account of, even by Congregational writers, although Dr. Dale, in his *Manual of Congregational Principles*, gives its true position and importance. They are (1) That every member of a Church must profess, and must be assumed, to be a spiritual believer in Christ Jesus, a believer "renewed in the spirit of his mind," and accepted as such by the fellowship of the Church. (2) That the members of every Christian Church form one distinct collective assembly, self-governing, and independent of every other Church. (3) That the Church meeting as a spiritual republic is the fountain of all authority and official position in the Church; and that in regard to questions of Church government and discipline coming before the Church, each several Church member possesses equal rights with every other member.[2]

In commenting on Dale's principles, Rigg suggests that the first is the most important yet the least emphasized. Churches whose polity places the entire burden (or at least the major part of the burden) for being true and authentic Christian communities on the parish are consistent when they expect all members of local congregations (or at least those who deliberate and vote) to have spiritual competency (the term commonly used by Baptists is "soul competency"), which enables them to conduct their affairs in ways faithful to the gospel. No special class of leaders provides assurance or takes over the task of achieving a faithful witness.

The obligations and the burdens of making such a polity work as intended are not inconsiderable. It is easy enough to hold in principle that every member of the Christian community is responsible for living by the requirements of the gospel, but putting this principle into practice is not easy. It can lead to concern for personal rectitude (and perhaps for spiritual enthusiasms) rather than to

---

2. James H. Rigg, D.D., *A Comparative View of Church Organizations: Primitive and Protestant, with a Supplement on Methodist Successions and Methodist Union* (London: Charles H. Kelly, 1897), 162f. The book referred to in this passage was authored by R. W. Dale, LL.D., and published in 1884 by Quinta Press, Shropshire, England, under the title *A Manual of Congregational Principles*. It was reprinted in 1996 by the Conservative Congregational Christian Conference.

theological learning or scholarly acumen. Moreover, it would be difficult to prove that, as they operate in modern circumstances, free church polities are distinguished by a more apparent fidelity in church members than that in denominations with other polities.

The emergence of the free church movement in the sixteenth and seventeenth centuries was in no small measure a reaction against politically established and centrally controlled religion. The freedom sought by the groups that formed this movement had two dimensions. One dimension involved independence from control by political authorities; the other dimension sought independence from ecclesiastical authorities. Not all congregationalism has been equally adamant about both of these dimensions. Some groups with congregational governance, in the United States at least, have repudiated the idea of an established church more consistently than others. Some have been especially conscious of their heritage in the left wing of the Reformation (which generally disapproved of politically established religion); others have kept in mind their heritage in Puritanism (willing to be the established religion wherever it managed to gain the power to do so).

Some congregational groups have insisted so strongly on the freedom and autonomy of the local community that they have deliberately refrained from joining efforts to become something like a denomination. I look at these groups in chapter 9. In this chapter, the concern is with associational congregationalism—with polities that affirm the freedom of the local parish to conduct its affairs yet that utilize associations of local parishes to accomplish specific objectives (such as cooperative mission work). Such associations may also provide local parishes with greater collegial support and a more impressive denominational identity than one community could have by itself. This pattern has been most fully evident in the polities of Congregational and Baptist denominations. In these denominations, local congregations form associations that do much to carry the weight of denominational identity. Although such associations do not control local congregations in the same ways or to the same extent as such control operates in the polities discussed above, they can offer special opportunities to achieve mutual covenantal responsibility.

THE UNITED CHURCH OF CHRIST

Although the terms *episcopal* and *presbyterian* are still widely used, it has been nearly fifty years since *congregational* has been used to name a major denomination.[3] This is because, during the 1940s and early 1950s, the denomination called Congregational Christian Churches held extensive negotiations with the Evangelical and Reformed Church (both groups having been created earlier by mergers) to form the United Church of Christ, which was officially founded in 1957. This organic union brought together a denomination in which a General Synod (subject to concurrence of its regional synods) had the power to take actions binding on local churches, with a denomination in which the actions of its General Council were merely advisory to local congregations. This union is sometimes referred to as "combining a church with churches." On the "church" side, the merger needed to be ratified only by central governing bodies; on the "churches" side, it had to be accepted by a majority vote of individual congregations. At the time, many people doubted such a union was possible—combining, as it did, elements of presbyterian and congregational polities—but it has resulted in a major body with strong denominational identity and a highly functional example of effective associational congregationalism. Many members of the United Church of Christ cherish this mutuality and regard it as more distinctive of the denomination than local autonomy.[4]

Article III of the Constitution of the United Church of Christ makes it clear that decision making is to be consultative and collaborative among all parts of the church's structure. Article IV declares that officers of the church are to meet as peers. Both of these articles are safeguards against development of a hierarchical order. Not only does the UCC constitution guard against hierarchical control, but the ethos of the denomination demonstrates that congregational polity, not infrequently found in theologically conservative groups, can be associated with generally liberal the-

---

3. The term *congregational* is still used by some small groups that refused to enter the merger that created the United Church of Christ.

4. See Reuben A. Shears II, "A Covenant Polity," in *Theology and Identity: Traditions, Movements, and Polity in the United Church of Christ,* ed. Daniel L. Johnson and Charles Hambrick-Stowe (Cleveland: United Church Press, 1990), 67–77.

ology, open church practice, and forward-looking social agendas. Not only was the United Church of Christ one of the first major denominations to encourage the ordination of women, but it is one of the few currently to permit the ordination of practicing gays and lesbians who are qualified to be ministers. It also has a history of liberal social witness pronouncements. These are aspects of a strong ethos of united witness and united effort.[5]

Nevertheless, the local congregation is the starting point for the polity of the United Church of Christ. The autonomy of the local congregation is protected by this strong constitutional language from Article V, section 18. "The autonomy of the Local Church is inherent and modifiable only by its own action." The governance of the local parish is carried on by a board of deacons, which has responsibility for spiritual matters, and by a board of trustees, which has responsibility for the finances and property. Both are elected by the congregation and function according to the provisions of the constitution or bylaws of the local parish. Tensions can develop between these two groups, each of which can meet by itself and create its own agenda. There is also a churchwide council consisting of the officers and chairpersons of the congregation's committees. There is no office of elder in this polity, nor are local parishes subject to supervision by a higher authority.

Congregations come together with other congregations to form an *association*. Ordained ministers who work in the area but who do not pastor churches are also members of the association as well as members of local churches. Associations are regional bodies that range in size from counties to parts of states. Each association writes its own constitution, even as each congregation makes many decisions on its own. The idea of freedom central to congregationally governed churches is thereby upheld by this aspect of the polity.

An Association elects its own officers, and it elects or appoints such committees as it deems necessary for the transaction of its business and the correlation of its work with that of the Confer-

---

5. A group of churches with congregational polity like that of the UCC but holding conservative theological and social views has formed a different national body, called the Conservative Congregational Christian Conference.

ence and the General Synod [explained below]. It determines its own method for securing financial support. It is concerned with the welfare of all local churches within its boundaries, and seeks ways and means to assist them when they are undergoing unusual difficulties requiring help beyond their own resources. It offers encouragement, guidance, and assistance in the organization of new local churches, and, with the counsel of the Conference, receives local churches into the United Church of Christ.[6]

The same ministers and churches also belong to *conferences,* which cover larger areas (such as states or contiguous states) than associations. These bodies provide fellowship and mutual support among congregations; they undertake joint projects that would be too large for individual parishes or local associations to manage; and they help provide a denominational reality that moves from the bottom up. Both associations and conferences derive their being from the congregations which come together to form them. The membership of ministers is not transferred from the local church to the associations or conferences. Indeed, in keeping with the congregational premise that ministers are part of the local body they are called to serve, all ministers have membership in congregations.[7] There is no prohibition, as in Presbyterian polity, of a minister without a parish, who attends a particular church, being on the membership roll or serving on one of its committees.

The main official of the conference is called a *conference minister* (although the term *president* is used in some conferences). The position does not involve a higher order of ministry or carry life tenure. Although it may sound strange, the administrative and pastoral work of the conference minister may be somewhat analogous to that of a pastoral bishop. The effectiveness of the office depends largely on persuasion rather than control. The office of conference minister must be held by an ordained person authorized for sacerdotal ministry in and on behalf of the whole church. While

---

6. Douglas Horton, *The United Church of Christ: Its Origins, Organization, and Role in the World Today* (New York: Thomas Nelson and Sons, 1962), 171.

7. Interestingly, as the United Church of Christ has worked out ministerial exchanges with denominations such as the Presbyterians, Evangelical Lutherans, and Reformed Church in America, UCC ministers become members of the local churches they serve—even those in other denominations—whereas ministers in those denominations do not.

the power of ordination is not lodged in the conference minister in the same way as in a bishop, the conference minister, like a bishop, participates in ordinations as a visible symbol of the church's unity.

The national body is called the General Synod. The term came from the Evangelical and Reformed tradition, even as the term *association* came from the Congregational Christian side. The synod is composed of many constituencies: elected delegates from the conferences; representatives of the agencies that conduct denominational affairs (called covenanted ministries); and other representatives. While in some polities a synod has controlling power, in the United Church of Christ, the constitution explicitly prohibits the synod from interfering with the autonomy of the conferences, associations, and local churches, or impairing their right to acquire, own, manage, and dispose of property and funds.

The General Synod elects the individuals who serve as officers of the church: a general minister and president; an associate general minister; an executive minister for local church ministries; an executive minister for wider church ministries; and an executive minister for justice and witness ministries. It may also elect other officers. These officers serve as a collegium. The General Synod also chooses a moderator to preside over its next meeting, assisted by two assistant moderators. An *executive council* has the power to act on behalf of the General Synod between its biennial meetings.

The General Synod, working in covenanted collegiality with interested constituencies in the church, establishes the major boards and agencies that carry on the work of the church and that provide its most visible denominational identity. It can receive funds for churchwide endeavors, and it bears responsibility for relationships with other churches and ecumenical agencies. The United Church of Christ, reflecting its own origins, is generally in the forefront of ecumenical efforts.

ASSOCIATIONAL ASPECTS OF THE UCC

The polity of the United Church of Christ exhibits its associational aspect in two ways. Each association has the power to determine whether to confer membership status on any congregation. It also determines, confers, and verifies ministerial standing within the denomination—one of its most important functions. Although the United Church strongly upholds the priesthood of all believers, and affirms that the laity have an apostolic role as important as the clergy's role, it makes special efforts to see that the church has a learned ministry. Three forms exist for the ministry—ordained, licensed, and commissioned. The *ordained ministry* consists of persons who have been ordained to ongoing preaching of the gospel, administration of sacraments and other rites of the church, and exercise of pastoral care and leadership. *Licensed ministers,* who are not necessarily ordained, can perform these functions for a designated period under supervision of the association. *Commissioned ministers,* who may be laypersons, carry on other church-related activities. All three forms carry voting membership in the association. They are not, however, steps in a hierarchy.

A local church can call and ordain persons to ministry without being credentialed by the association. However, ordinations authorized and carried out only by local parishes provide no standing in the church as a whole and have not been widely practiced since the early days of New England Congregationalism.

The first step in seeking ordination in the United Church of Christ is to come under care of the association. This involves examination on fitness and motives for seeking to become a minister. Those accepted are supported and supervised in their formal preparation, which generally includes graduation from both college and seminary. Although this has been the normal pattern, the UCC increasingly acknowledges the validity of other forms of preparation or experience as fitting persons for ministry. When a person nears the end of seminary training, or seeks ordination on the basis of special experience and skills, she or he prepares a paper setting forth his or her religious experience and understanding of basic theological affirmations. On the basis of this paper, the candidate is examined by the association's Committee on the Ministry. There is probably less emphasis in this examination on proving orthodoxy than on demonstrating deep religious motivations and on understanding the meaning of faith. In this process, as described many years ago, "the Church seeks to learn the candidate's own insights into the Gospel. Here there is a two-way motion of the spirit, the church seeking to understand the man [*sic*] and the man seeking to understanding the church, all within their mutual commitment to God as he reveals himself in Christ."[8] Laity have a part in examining the candidate's suitability. Ordination is by the laying on of hands of ministers of the association, a group of whom assemble for the service, and often by the hands of some layperson or laypersons delegated for the function.

The way candidates are examined for ordination is a clue to the way theology is viewed in the United Church of Christ. There is freedom to understand the gospel and the Christian life in ways that are especially meaningful for the individual—though such beliefs are to be informed by the ancient creeds of the church and the insights of the reformers. Many individual congregations write and adopt their own covenants of purpose. Richness of understanding tends to be valued more than theological correctness. At times, a desire has arisen for a more explicit identification of foundational beliefs. Early in the life of the new denomination, a committee was appointed to draw up a brief statement of faith as a means of witnessing to common convictions. It was decided that the statement would not be used for testing the orthodoxy of members. The result was a statement of faith designed for liturgical use. Many members of the church have found that its cadences and affirmations lift the heart more than bind the mind. That the language of this statement has been revised for inclusiveness shows that it is part of a dynamic process of growth and development. It is a testimonial rather than a test of faith.

> We believe in you, O God, Eternal Spirit,
> God of our Savior Jesus Christ, and our God,
> and to your deeds we testify:
> You call the worlds into being,
> create persons in your own image,
> and set before each one the ways of life and death.
> You seek in holy love to save all people from aimlessness and sin.
> You judge people and nations by your righteous will
> declared through prophets and apostles.
> In Jesus Christ, the man of Nazareth, our crucified and risen
> Savior,

---

8. Horton, *United Church of Christ,* 142.

you have come to us
and shared our common lot,
conquering sin and death,
and reconciling the world to yourself.

You bestow upon us your Holy Spirit,
    creating and renewing the Church of Jesus Christ,
    binding in covenant faithful people of all ages, tongues,
        and races.

You call us into your church
    to accept the cost and joy of discipleship,
    to be your servants in the service of others,
    to proclaim the gospel to all the world
    and resist the powers of evil,
    to share in Christ's baptism and eat at his table,
    to join him in his passion and victory.

You promise to all who trust you
    forgiveness of sins and fullness of grace,
    courage in the struggle for justice and peace,
    your presence in trial and rejoicing,
    and eternal life in your realm which has no end.

Blessing and honor, glory and power, be unto you. Amen.[9]

The dialectical tension between the freedom of local congregations and the impulse to have a corporate denominational identity
is not easy to maintain. Those who work in the denomination's
bureaucracy must deal with such tensions when they arise between
constituencies. "Pressures mount when those various constituencies want their views of proper beliefs and practices to be adopted
by the denomination as a whole."[10] That tension has been characteristic of the United Church of Christ from its beginning, and it is
dealt with creatively and with goodwill in an ethos characterized
equally by freedom and covenanted mutuality.

9. United Church of Christ Statement of Faith in the Form of a Doxology. Approved
by the Executive Council in 1981 for use in connection with the twenty-fifth anniversary
of the United Church of Christ.

10. W. Widrick Schroeder, "The United Church of Christ: The Quest for Denominational Identity and the Limits of Pluralism," in *The United Church of Christ: Studies in
Identity and Polity,* ed. Dorothy C. Bass and Kenneth B. Smith (Chicago: Exploration Press,
1987), 25.

BAPTIST TRADITIONS

The other major example of associational congregationalism is provided by Baptist churches. The principles of the Baptist doctrine of the church, as found in *A Baptist Manual of Polity and Practice*, suggest the importance of both the local congregation and of the associational dimension.

The most distinctive emphasis of the early Baptists was their threefold formulation addressing the relationship of the church to the churches:

1. They believed that the latter should reproduce, as nearly as possible in this imperfect world, the life of faith, obedience, and fellowship which characterizes the former. To this end they rejected infant baptism, insisting upon believer's baptism.

2. Holding firmly to the primacy of the universal church, they also insisted that each individual church represented the larger church in its locality, and had all necessary powers of self-government.

3. At the same time, they devised ways to express the interdependence of local churches, so that the tendency to an isolated self-sufficiency would be avoided. Around these three points the Baptist doctrine of the church revolved.[11]

The foundational unit of Baptist ecclesiology is the local congregation. While the local congregation enjoys the right to govern its own affairs—to admit (and dismiss) members, to call (and, if necessary, ordain) its own ministers, to possess (or dispose of) its own property, and to write its own covenants of purpose (which in some sense serve as doctrinal standards)—most Baptist churches conform to recognizable patterns that do much to counteract the otherwise centrifugal consequences that might flow from purely local decision making. To be sure, there are often differences (particularly in theological stance) between one local Baptist church and another, or between one Baptist association and other Baptist associations. Yet churches within the various Baptist associations have a similar set of worship practices (marked by fervor and informality). Although this similarity in posture and

---

11. Norman H. Maring and Winthrop S. Hudson, *A Baptist Manual of Polity and Practice: Revised Edition* (Valley Forge, Pa.: Judson Press, 1991), 38.

practice is voluntary, it is sufficiently in evidence to give Baptists a recognizable identity, despite the differences.

The largest Baptist denominations are the Southern Baptist Convention, the three African American denominations (National Baptists, Progressive National Baptists, and National Baptists USA), and the American Baptist Churches USA (successor to the Northern Baptist Convention and still colloquially called "northern Baptists"). But there are more than two dozen other Baptist groups. Although, in some groups of Baptists, congregational freedom is associated, as in the United Church of Christ, with tolerance of theological diversity and support for ecumenical cooperation, in many groups the reverse is the case. Theological rigidity is prevalent and ecumenical cooperation frowned upon. The contrast between the United Church of Christ and the conservative Baptist groups (as well as between liberal and conservative Baptists) is a good example of how very different characteristics can come from generally similar polities.

The typical local Baptist congregation makes decisions about a number of issues. Membership, for instance, is granted by congregational action. Sometimes, as in much past practice, this involves meeting newcomers at a gathering of the entire church, inquiring into their Christian experience, requiring baptism by immersion, and taking a vote of members present while the newcomer is temporarily excused. This is no longer a necessary scenario. Today it is more usual for the deacons—as the governing board of the local church—to meet with those seeking membership and to recommend them to the congregation for approval (rejection of those recommended is rare).

Variations exist within this basic pattern. Some Baptist churches grant full membership only to those who have been, or who agree to be, baptized by immersion. Others allow persons who do not meet this standard to become associate, but not full, members. Still others practice open membership, giving full status to persons previously baptized according to the practice of their previous denomination. The choice among these options is a local decision, although the choice is apt to be a clue to a church's theological stance.

With respect to the selection and authorization of ministerial

leadership, each church is constitutionally free to choose its ministers and even to ordain them. Baptist ministers—unlike Episcopal,
Methodist, or Presbyterian clergy—are members of the congregations they serve. Just as they are called by the local church,
they may be dismissed by vote. Time, however, has modified this
local autonomy. The status of Baptist ministers is now monitored
(though not determined) by Baptist associations. Local churches
usually seek the advice and counsel of the association in calling ministers. The status of ministers is enhanced by having their
ordinations performed by the association. The association sets educational expectations; examines candidates for competency and
orthodoxy; assists local congregations in the service of ordination; and even enters as a friendly interlocutor if tensions develop
between a congregation and its minister.

The Role of the Association

The association helps introduce orderliness into a process that
could be quite random. But it nevertheless allows churches to call
(or retain) pastors who would not be approved by the association. For example, the Southern Baptist Convention has recently
codified a provision that only men can serve as pastors.[12] This
action is a move by conservatives, who have come to control the
Southern Baptists, to make opposition to female ministers explicit
and weighty rather than a matter of custom. But even if this stricture against women pastors is part of the Southern Baptists' belief
statement, local churches may still have women pastors, and the
Convention cannot stop them. The Convention's stand, however,
must be overridden with caution, even if it is not a binding rule.

Individual churches can own their property and dispose of it
as they see fit. Some associations try to persuade churches to
agree to a provision in their local constitutions that, in the case
of dissolution, property will be distributed to the denominational
association or to one of its agencies. That does not, however, settle
property issues if the church splits and each side wants to receive
its share.

---

12. *The Daily Press*, Hampton, Virginia, June 11, 2000, A12.

Local churches also decide on their own covenants of purpose. These statements articulate the general commitments of the local congregation and frequently involve matters of practice as well as belief. A local church could write a covenant that emphasizes service to neighbor and concern for the poor and outcast as its central purpose, or it could write a covenant that stipulates conservative theological principles and restrictions on lifestyles. Writing these covenants when churches are organized, or revising them as conditions change, does require thought and negotiation that can raise awareness of the sacred obligations entailed in church membership.

But the associational principle has significance in this area as in other matters. Many congregations adopt a covenant in general circulation within the denomination. The following covenant is the most common among Baptists today.

Having been led, as we believe, by the Spirit, to receive the Lord Jesus Christ as our Savior, and on the profession of our faith having been baptized in the name of the Father, and of the Son, and of the Holy Spirit, we do now in the presence of God and this assembly most solemnly and joyfully enter into covenant with one another, as one body in Christ.

We engage, therefore, by the aid of the Holy Spirit, to walk together in Christian love, to strive for the advancement of this church in knowledge, holiness, and comfort; to promote its prosperity and spirituality, to sustain its worship, ordinances, discipline, and doctrines; to contribute cheerfully and regularly to the support of the ministry, the expenses of the church, the relief of the poor, and the spread of the gospel throughout all nations.

We also engage to maintain as far as possible family and secret devotion; to teach our children the Christian truths; to seek the salvation of our kindred and acquaintances; to walk circumspectly in the world; to be just in our dealings, faithful in our engagements, exemplary in our deportment, and zealous in our efforts to advance the kingdom of our Savior.

We further engage to watch over one another in Christian love; to remember each other in prayer; to aid each other in sickness and distress; to cultivate Christian sympathy in feeling and courtesy in speech; to be slow to take offense but always ready for reconciliation, and mindful of the rules of our Savior to secure it without delay.

We moreover engage that, when we remove from this place, we will as soon as possible unite with some other church where we can carry out the spirit of the covenant and the principles of God's Word.[13]

The general provisions of this covenant are rich in Christian discipleship. This document sets forth a remarkable ideal. However, although many Baptists have agreed to it, the family (or families) of Baptist churches are not free from theological controversy, nor are Baptists unique in the extent to which their members achieve spiritual discipline.

FACING CONTROVERSY

As with connectional congregationalism, creation of the association offers the possibility for controversy. When individual churches differ in theology or practice, it is natural for them to believe that their interpretation of the gospel should characterize all churches in the denomination. The election of delegates to the Convention becomes politicized. In recent years, the Southern Baptist Convention has witnessed a concerted effort by fundamentalists to obtain control. When they obtain a voting majority, they are in a position to control functions directly supported by the Convention—such as mission work or theological seminaries. Such control can be exercised directly over aspects of the church's life created and maintained by the Convention, but pressure on individual congregations to conform to the Convention's prevailing outlook also increases, even though such influence is indirect and theoretically nonbinding.

Since provisions for supervising denominational programs are not explicit in Baptist polity, Convention officials find ways to achieve results without creating a backlash. Many years ago, a study of these officials created considerable stir. In this study, Paul Harrison, a theologian and sociologist, examined how denominational officials in what was then the Northern Baptist Convention,

---

13. Maring and Hudson, *Baptist Manual of Polity and Practice*, 254f.

usually regarded as more liberal and open than its southern coun-terpart, "gained greater power over the activities of the churches than has ever been recognized as legitimate by the official apolo-gists for the Baptist movement."[14] Harrison distinguished between "a formal system of authority," what I have designated as explicit provisions for control, and an "informal system of power." Re-jecting the former required officials who bear responsibilities for shaping denominational life to resort to the latter. Much of this informal control requires charismatic qualities that depend on per-sonal influence and negotiating acumen. Although such control develops over time and by virtue of skillful interactions, this power is not without consequences. According to Harrison,

> [A]lthough informal, the power of executives may reach startling proportions. Modern Baptist emphasis upon ultimate authority of the individual believer, the authority of the local church, and the corresponding "containment" of the authority of the execu-tive professionals resulted in unanticipated consequences. Being permitted nothing more, at least on the official level, than an in-strumental function with no ecclesiastical authority, the executives were forced to substitute informal power for official authority. In individual cases, this can far exceed the power of many executives or ecclesiastical officers of the "authoritarian" religious orders.[15]

An example of the expanding power of denominational officials is a 1999 case in which a professional staff member of National Ministries of the American Baptist Churches USA, responsible for corporate responsibility and economic justice, was asked to resign by the executive director. The executive's action significantly al-tered the stance and program of the church without a decision by a representative body.

Baptist churches, particularly in the South, are among the most numerous and possibly fastest-growing church groups in contem-porary America. Local decision making enables them to adapt to the mores and circumstances of local cultures more easily

---

14. Paul M. Harrison, *Authority and Power in the Free Church Tradition: A Social Case Study of the American Baptist Convention* (Princeton, N.J.: Princeton University Press, 1959), 7.

15. Ibid., 94.

than more fully structured denominations adhering to traditional patterns.

Baptists are not restricted by allegiance to historic or formal practices in worship. Baptist congregations assume many levels of sophistication, from storefronts or whitewashed concrete-block shacks established by evangelists with little theological training to major churches with highly trained ministers and elaborate edifices. They vary widely in theological orientation, from liberal congregations (usually, but not always, in the North) to some of the most adamant advocates of biblical literalism and restrictive expectations regarding private moral behavior. Their ministers are accorded contrasting levels of allegiance, from the high level of regard and obedience often shown pastors in black Baptist churches (some of whom are even called "bishop" as a mark of respect) to far more casual treatment elsewhere. Such treatment is afforded pastors in churches in which a minister is looked on as a kind of domesticated caretaker, available on request to provide for church members' spiritual benefit.

Despite some significant social witness and the fact that some of the most effective and best-known leaders of social change have been Baptists, the polity of this tradition is not strongly suited to protect prophetic leadership. This is especially true where a congregation is composed of persons more bound to the mores of a culture than responsive to the transformative expectations of the gospel.

Resources on Associational Congregationalism

For Understanding the United Church of Christ

Bass, Dorothy C., and Kenneth D. Smith, eds. *The United Church of Christ: Studies in Identity and Polity.* Chicago: Exposition Press, 1987.

Book of Worship of the United Church of Christ. New York: Office for Church Life and Leadership, 1986.

Constitution and Bylaws of the United Church of Christ. Cleveland: Executive Council of the United Church of Christ, 2000. http://www.ucc.org/aboutus/constitution.htm [downloads in PDF format].

Council for Church and Ministry, the United Church of Christ. *The Manual of the Ministry in the United Church of Christ.* Rev. ed. New York: Office for Church Life and Leadership, 1986.

Fauth, Robert T. *So You Are a Church Member.* Revised and updated edition. Cleveland: United Church Press, 1975.

Horton, Douglas. *The United Church of Christ: Its Origins, Organization, and Role in the World Today.* New York: Thomas Nelson and Sons, 1962.

Johnson, Daniel L., and Charles Hambrick-Stowe, eds. *Theology and Identity: Traditions, Movements, and Polity in the United Church of Christ.* Cleveland: United Church Press, 1990.

For Understanding Baptist Churches

Brackney, William H., ed. *The Baptists.* Westport, Conn.: Greenwood Press, 1988.

Deweese, Charles W. *Baptist Church Covenants.* Nashville: Broadman Press, 1990.

Harrison, Paul M. *Authority and Power in the Free Church Tradition: A Social Case Study of the American Baptist Convention.* Princeton, N.J.: Princeton University Press, 1959.

Hudson, Winthrop S., ed. *Baptist Concepts of the Church.* Valley Forge, Pa.: Judson Press, 1959.

Leonard, Bill. *God's Last and Best Hope: The Fragmentation of the SBC.* Grand Rapids, Mich.: Eerdmans, 1990.

————, ed. *Dictionary of Baptists in America.* Downers Grove, Ill.: InterVarsity Press, 1994.

Maring, Norman H., and Winthrop S. Hudson. *A Baptist Manual of Polity and Practice.* Rev. ed. Valley Forge, Pa.: Judson Press, 1991.

Recommended Procedures for Ordination, Commissioning, and Recognition for the Christian Ministry in the American Baptist Churches. Valley Forge, Pa., 1990.

Shurden, Walter B. *Associationalism among Baptists in America.* New York: Arno Press, 1980.

Sullivan, James L. *Baptist Polity as I See It.* Rev. ed. Nashville: Broadman and Holman, 1998.

————. *Southern Baptist Polity at Work in a Church.* Nashville: Convention Press, 1987.

9

CONGREGATIONS WITHOUT OVERSTRUCTURES

W E COME TO WAYS of thinking about ecclesiastical governance that take congregational autonomy to what is
possibly its ultimate expression—namely, that local gatherings of
believers have no need to construct systems of church law in
order to relate to one another structurally. In the early eighteenth
century, a number of churches organized in New England and
took the simple designation, "Christian Churches." One of their
members described their intentions: "We mean to be New Testament Christians without any sectarian name connected with
it, without any sectarian creeds, articles, or confessions, or discipline to eliminate the scripture.... It is our design to remain free
from all human laws, considerations, and unscriptural combina-
tions, and to stand fast in the liberty wherewith Christ has made
us free."[1]

Although this statement may sound like the repudiation of
polity, it represents an effort to govern church life by an alternative vision, which takes the place of polity in the usual sense.
The idea constitutes a form of governance, but not governance in
the sense found in most traditions. This vision has had considerable appeal, especially in the United States, and there have been
serious efforts to develop churches according to its principles. In
one expression, it is alleged that Christians will come together
only if they abandon governance that keeps them separated and
restore the church to the way it was in New Testament times.

---

1. Quoted in Hampton Adams, *Why I Am a Disciple of Christ* (New York: Thomas
Nelson and Sons, 1957), 23f.

The early experience of what is now called the Christian Church (Disciples of Christ) was an effort to seek unity by repudiating structures not found in the biblical account of the New Testament church. It started with the idea of being a movement that all Christians could readily embrace, not a denomination. Its later development suggests the difficulties inherent in the early efforts; it ended by restructuring itself into a Protestant body with many of the features of associational congregationalism.

THE ORIGINS OF THE CHRISTIAN CHURCH (DISCIPLES OF CHRIST)

To understand the Christian Church (Disciples of Christ), it is necessary to know its origins. At the beginning of the nineteenth century, a feeling developed in many places that all patterns of church governance since New Testament times (such as those described in previous chapters) were barriers to the unity Christians have in Christ. Many persons were disenchanted with the manner in which churches used creeds and polities to restrict freedom and to demand conformity to requirements that, in their view, had no biblical warrant.

Those so oriented wanted to restore the New Testament church in its pristine purity, to enjoy the liberty they believed Christ had offered, and to replace the laws and practices that churches had developed subsequently with the liberty they believed to be possible in Christ. The founders of movements that eventually became the Christian Church (Disciples of Christ) shared this impulse, typically because they had experienced repression from traditional denominations or had seen others treated harshly by ecclesiastical authority.

One such leader was Barton W. Stone, a Presbyterian clergyman who started his ministerial career as a supply preacher in Kentucky in 1796. Stone was influenced by movements that favored religious toleration and also by revivalism, which emphasized conversion as the heartfelt decision of the individual. When two of his fellow Presbyterians were charged with disloyalty to the Westminster Confession of Faith—because they preached that Christ had died for all persons and not merely for the elect—Stone joined five other ministers in withdrawing from the Presbyterian Synod of Kentucky and in setting up their own presbytery.

In less than a year, this group decided to disband the new presbytery. The move to disband was prompted by their feeling that an effort was needed to restore the purity of the New Testament church—free from the encumbrances of governance that had hobbled the traditional churches. The gatherings founded by Stone called themselves "Christian Churches" and came to include some ten thousand followers in less than thirty years.[2]

Meanwhile, Thomas Campbell, a Scotch-Irish Presbyterian disillusioned with the divisiveness taking place among various Presbyterian groups in Ireland, immigrated to Pennsylvania. Assigned to preach on the frontier in southwestern Pennsylvania, he became involved in a controversy with the presbytery for favoring open admission to the Lord's Supper. He withdrew to form a Christian association in Washington, Pennsylvania, which took as its motto, "Where the Scriptures speak, we speak; where the Scriptures are silent, we are silent." He also wrote *Declaration and Address*, which set forth his views and which would become an influential piece for the movement to follow.

Alexander Campbell, the son of Thomas, was studying for the ministry in Glasgow, Scotland, where he was influenced by the Haldane movement, which advocated a return to primitive Christianity (as known in the New Testament) as a way of overcoming denominational divisions. Alexander came to the United States, discovered the similarity between his father's views and those of the Haldanes, and joined his father in establishing a self-governing congregation that observed the Lord's Supper on a weekly basis. The younger Campbell preached a sermon at one of the early meetings that articulated the anti-institutional premise:

> [I]gnorance and superstition, enthusiasm and fanaticism are the fruits of these human institutions which have displaced the Bible or refused to admit it as its own interpreter. We commence our career as a church under the banner of *"The Bible, the whole Bible, and nothing but the Bible,"* as the standard of our religious

2. This account based on Mark G. Toulouse, *Joined in Discipleship: The Shaping of Contemporary Disciples Identity* (St. Louis: Chalice Press, 1997), 25f.

faith and practice.... Our inferences and opinions are our own.
...Christians are the sons of liberty—the Lord's freed men.[3]

Campbell's congregation later decided that the Bible required believer's baptism by immersion and entered a cooperative relationship with Baptist groups; the relationship lasted several years and gave quasi-denominational standing to Campbell's group. But, as time went on, the Baptists insisted on using a confession of faith as a test of orthodoxy, and the relationship ruptured. Theologically, although appealing to the Bible as the sole authority, Campbell was what today would be called a liberal rather than a conservative—and certainly not a fundamentalist. His thinking reflected the Enlightenment with its emphasis on reason and empirical experience and the American ideal of liberty. In order to avoid being considered a denomination, the movement called itself "The Disciples of Christ."

These two groups, the group calling itself Christians and the group calling itself Disciples, came together in 1832 and grew almost tenfold in the next three decades, and another fivefold by the end of the nineteenth century. It called itself by both names, the Christian Church and Disciples of Christ, and this dual designation has lasted to the present. Although determined initially not to institutionalize, the Christian Church (Disciples of Christ) became a distinct group of Christians, particularly in the Midwest. It embraced the principle of diversity as a corollary of freedom and sought Christian unity as a mandate of the gospel—hoping thereby to restore the reality of the New Testament church. It also contended that its approach was a means of overcoming the divisions caused by the differences in church governance.

The union of the followers of Barton Stone with the followers of the Campbells found that its member churches could work together. It created a mission agency, the American Christian Missionary Society. The creation of this society was not without controversy, however, for some felt the organization was a move toward becoming a denomination—even though it could exercise no authority over constituent congregations.

---

3. Ibid., 28.

Still greater differences arose over reading scripture as the basis for belief and practice. The idea that scripture interprets itself did not create a common mind. Alternative readings of the New Testament as a basis for restoring the church in its purity produced differing judgments as to what was permitted (or required) and what was prohibited. One side continued to hold that freedom is a central element, to reject the use of creeds as tests of fidelity, and to support academic freedom in church-related colleges and universities. Another side concluded that the use of organs (or other instrumental accompaniment for congregational singing) had no New Testament warrant and should not be allowed in worship. Moreover, it held that the cooperative deployment of missionaries through missionary societies was not authorized by New Testament practice. The conservative group became uneasy about the theological openness in academic institutions under church auspices.

These two sides parted early in the nineteenth century. The group reading New Testament practice most stringently, which took the name Churches of Christ, was heavily associated with the agrarian culture of the southern states. Unable to find common ground with the larger group called Disciples, it continued to insist on a radical view of congregational autonomy, to oppose instrumental music in worship, and to repudiate organizational cooperation through missionary societies.

The Disciples continued to grow in numbers. But controversy arose over whether the Disciples, opposed to organizing themselves into a denomination, should recognize the legitimacy of churches that did. One group, which continued under the name Disciples, favored such recognition. Another group, which came to be known as the Independents, opposed such a concession to denominationalism, feeling that it abandoned the Disciples' contention that Christian unity should be sought through apostolic faith as revealed in the New Testament. The division took the form not of two organized groups in battle, but of two parties separated, like liberal and conservative parties in many denominations at the time.[4]

---

4. This history of these movements is summarized in D. Newell Williams, ed., *A Case*

COMMON PRACTICES

Several practices have been common to these related movements, even though the autonomy of local congregations has allowed for variation. One of the distinguishing practices has been believers' baptism by immersion, adopted because it was felt to have been the pattern in New Testament times. The practice of immersion is considered to have profound symbolic meaning in representing the death and resurrection of Christ. Immersion therefore is strongly recommended for all persons wishing to join a congregation and required to join many congregations. But Disciples do not necessarily regard other forms of baptism as invalid. As in many Baptist churches, some congregations require re-baptism by immersion for persons coming from another denomination, but others (probably the majority) do not. Moreover, Disciples have never let the matter interfere with cooperation with other Christian groups, even though profoundly convinced of its importance in their own practice. (I know of one Disciples minister who agreed to be the godfather at an infant baptism involving the child of close friends.)

Another distinguishing practice came to be the weekly celebration of the Lord's Supper. Observance of this sacrament, however, was generally placed in the hands of lay elders or other lay members of the congregation. In some congregations, the minister is not present at the communion table. The lay elders expound briefly on the meaning of this ritual and offer a prayer or prayers of thanksgiving they have composed themselves (though they have the freedom to use selections from a treasury of prayers). Deacons distribute the bread and wine to the congregation in their seats. There is no requirement for words of institution, which have such a familiar ring to most traditions, but neither is there a prohibition of their use.

That elders rather than the minister have the key role at the communion table, or that elders are always at the communion table whether or not the minister is present, is a clue to how the Christian Church views the ministry. There has been a distinct effort to underscore the parity of laity and clergy and to prevent

Study of Mainstream Protestantism: The Disciples' Relation to American Culture, 1880–1989 (Grand Rapids, Mich.: Eerdmans; St. Louis: Chalice Press, 1991), 3–10.

the development of a clerical class. Moreover, each congregation is theoretically free to choose persons from its own ranks (or from outside) and to set them apart by the laying on of hands. At times this practice has resulted in untrained persons entering the ministry. But the movement over time has been decidedly against such local practice. The Disciples as a whole have sought to have a learned ministry, meaning that theological training is expected. State organizations (called regions) have arisen, with the important function of providing intercongregational participation in examining potential ministers, encouraging their adequate preparation, and participating in their ordination. Ordination is for functional leadership and does not carry sacerdotal powers.

The organization of local churches has not followed a mandated pattern. It has usually involved elders and deacons; there were separate deacons and deaconesses at first, but one diaconate since 1895. In many parishes, the elders are on call as minister's advisers when a crisis develops, but they otherwise do not exercise authority. The local elders are basically nonstipendiary ministers, sharing spiritual leadership with the minister or providing leadership when a church has no pastor.[5] Members of the diaconate, together with others bearing special responsibilities, constitute an official board, responsible for different aspects of the congregation's life—worship, evangelism, missions, education, finance, and property. In some congregations there is also a board of trustees. In such cases, the trustees act as the legal agents of the congregation regarding finances and property; they do so by carrying out the decisions of the official board and of the congregation, rather than by assuming direction and control.[6] In 1955, the Christian Church (Disciples of Christ) made several studies of its reasons for being. In that report, the Disciples' basic ecclesiology was articulated in a statement stressing the positive role played by the gospel message in the church's formation:

> We scarcely can over-emphasize the importance of the Apostolic "kerygma" and the human response to it as determining the char-

---

5. See "The Ministry of the Disciples Elder," in Colbert S. Cartwright, *People of the Chalice: Disciples of Christ in Faith and Practice* (St. Louis: CBP Press, 1987), 37–44.

6. This description of the typical church organization is based on Adams, *Why I Am a Disciple*, 88–89.

acter of the church in New Testament times. From this constitutive principle flows the unity of the church. The response of men, let it be noted, was to the "kerygma." It is not to a creedal statement of faith, or to the theory of the atonement, or to a code of ethics, or to a church polity, or to a theory concerning the sacraments, or to an order of clergy, or to a theological explanation of the Christ-hood of Jesus. These matters came later—some of them after the church came into existence—but the response, by which humanly speaking, the church began, was to the "kerygma."[7]

A New Structure of Governance

For more than a century, the Disciples hoped to provide an alternative model to denominational governance—one involving response to the gospel rather than conformity to an institution. Many refused to speak of their group as a denomination. But in 1968, after seven years of discussion and study, an organization was approved that structured the Disciples of Christ in a more connectional way. Congregations continue to manage their own affairs, but they elect voting representatives to regional and national assemblies, much like many other denominations. It would probably be correct to state that this new structure places the Disciples within associational congregationalism.

There are thirty-six regional assemblies, and each determines how to manage its work and witness. They have an active role in judging the fitness of candidates for ordination, certify the standing of qualified ministers, and are involved in the call process by which ministers and churches come together. Their work is facilitated by regional ministers, who devote themselves full-time to administrative leadership.

The new structure also provides national bodies that elect officers for the denomination and govern the work of cooperative national ventures. A general board, half elected by the General Assembly and half by the regions, "meets annually, processes business going to the assembly, recommends policies, reviews the total program of the church, elects or confirms the governing boards of the various administrative units, and elects the committees of the

7. Cited in ibid., 70f.

General Assembly and the members of an administrative committee. One-third of general board members are ministers; the
remainder are laypersons."[8] An administrative committee of the
general board consists of up to forty members and meets twice
a year. The chief officer of the denomination, who provides both
pastoral care and executive oversight, is called the general minister
and president.

The preamble to the plan restructuring the Disciples was a brief
statement of faith, in format similar to that of the United Church
of Christ. The interesting feature of this statement is that it affirms
beliefs about Jesus Christ before it turns to beliefs concerning God
and the Holy Spirit. It also mentions baptism, while not specifying
a particular form, and the importance of the Lord's table.

The Christian Church (Disciples of Christ) has continued in
the forefront of ecumenical activity. As the church has changed,
however, so has its relationship to ecumenical bodies like the
National Council of Churches and World Council of Churches.
Instead of thinking of itself as an alternative to other polities, the
Disciples of Christ acts like a denomination with a polity of its
own, standing alongside polities of all other members of ecumenical organizations. Its polity thus becomes a matter to consider
as churches work toward fuller cooperation and the possibility of
greater unity.

LOCALLY INDEPENDENT CONGREGATIONS

Unlike the Campbellites, who were inspired by a vision of Christian unity, our society is filled with small religious gatherings with
little or no connection to any major body and not a great deal to
do with each other. These groups exist on their own terms and by
their capacity to attract followers.

Giving these groups a name is difficult. The phrase "sects
and cults" is frequently used, but two terms have had different meanings in scholarly discourse, and the phrase has acquired
a pejorative meaning in popular thinking. In polity, some sects

---

8. Frank S. Mead, *Handbook of Denominations in the United States*, revised by Samuel S.
Hill, new 10th ed. (Nashville: Abingdon Press, 1995), 97.

and some cults are connectional or ruled by a central figure; others are not. John Paul Williams used "nonecclesiastical spiritual movements" to describe groups that do not gain their chief impetus from an organization, but Williams described movements without churchly features, whereas many small, independent congregations have churchly characteristics.[9] Charles H. Libby has suggested the term *popular religiosity*, but his category covers a far broader phenomenon.[10] A recently published encyclopedia describes groups that fit this pattern as "Postdenominational." It suggests they are something of a countercultural reaction to organized religion.[11] While these groups are numerous they are also fragmented.

In terms of polity, they constitute local gatherings without overstructures. They are congregational without being denominational. In the yellow pages of one area, which lists churches according to denominational identity, one finds three categories: "Churches: Independent"; "Churches: Interdenominational"; and "Churches: Non-denominational." None of the churches listed— even those designated interdenominational—indicates association with a major Christian movement.

Most of these groups—if not all—suggest that congregational governance without overstructures differs from the idealistically motivated Campbellite movement and its aftermath. In this second version of congregationalism without overstructures, the freedom of the local congregation to "do its own thing" is taken for granted, and the necessity of formal polity or interparochial structures is either ignored or repudiated. There is little interest in Christian cooperation or unity. Individual gatherings of believers are considered free to set up their own standards of belief and conduct, subservient only to their own perception of God's will.

Whereas in the congregationalism without overstructures represented by the early Disciples, in which the repudiation of polity

---

9. John Paul Williams, *What Americans Believe and How They Worship* (New York and Evanston, Ill.: Harper and Row, 1962), 453–71.

10. Charles H. Libby, *Being Religious American Style: A History of Popular Religiosity in the United States* (Westport, Conn., and London: Greenwood Press, 1994).

11. See the entry "Postdenominational Church" written by Donald E. Miller in Wade Clark Roof, ed., *Contemporary American Religion*, vol. 2 (New York: Macmillan Reference USA, 2000), 540.

became a polity of its own, yearning deeply for the unity of all believers, in the second version, local autonomy provides an escape
from accountability beyond that of the local group. The many
small and unassociated groups that spring up around preaching and evangelizing—typically that of persons who set out on
their own because they believe that only intense religious fervor
is needed to legitimize a ministry—illustrate total independency.
Many of these groups are uninterested in relationship with other
groups or in becoming part of a more inclusive Christian movement. They are often formed as a result of privatized religious
entrepreneurship.

Anyone, particularly in Bible Belt country, can find groups with
names such as Apostolic Faith Church; Beyond the Veil Worship
Center; Church of the Way and Truth; Cornerstone Fellowship
Church; Church of the Living Word; City of Refuge Church;
Grace Bible Church; Holy Temple Church; Humble Beginnings
Interdenominational Ministry; Mercy and Trust Ministries; New
Life Church of God; Living Waters Christian Fellowship; Voice of
Victory Church; Church by the Bay.

These small, independent groups are served by persons who
generally designate themselves ministers or pastors, who may or
may not have scholarly credentials, who may or may not associate with local ministerial associations, who may or may not be
accountable to any ecclesiastical body other than the local flock
which attends their services and which contributes (in many cases
sacrificially) to their support. It is not hard to get certified as a
minister providing one does not care about the public credibility
of the certification. Mail-order degrees have long been offered to
those who will pay for them. It has become possible recently to go
online, to send one's name to a web site such as First International
Church of the Web,[12] and to be accorded the title of reverend
or even doctor of divinity. As long as our national constitution
protects the free exercise of religion, and as long as such activities are plausibly religious in character—which the courts usually
hold them to be—this kind of activity is free to proceed without
interference. The only assurance that such a process for certify-

---

12. http://ficotw.org

ing religious leaders will diminish is the capacity of the public to discern when leadership is thoroughly trained and professionally competent and when it is inadequate or fraudulent—respecting the former and rejecting the latter. That capacity in a land where learning about religion—if such learning happens at all—in a scholarly manner is confined to higher education, and takes place only in some institutions, is not in overabundance.

There is little need for, or concern about, the broader issues of polity in such communities. Some of these groups may even meet in private homes—as did many gatherings in New Testament times. It is possible that, to those accustomed to the structured quality of Jewish institutions in the time of Jesus, early Christian love feasts appeared as problematic as these groups do to us. The Christians who met in small groups were attacked because they were reported to eat flesh and drink blood—an idea that could very well appear scandalous if not understood in its experiential reality. Moreover, these groups may, in time, become parts of a more structured polity, but they presently constitute a form of complete local autonomy.

Religious entrepreneurship can also occur on the megachurch level. Once in a while the charismatic gifts and skillful appeal of a leader become sufficient to attract a large following, extended through use of the mass media. A large establishment is created with a major monetary intake and committed following. Not many such megagatherings make efforts to support ecumenical organizations, though some have large outreach ministries through the media. The majority are either fundamentalist or expound a version of Christianity that emphasizes something like positive thinking and individualistic spirituality. The ministers are in some cases members of mainline groups, but they do not make allegiance to the doctrine, practices, or ecclesiology of that group a controlling factor in determining how they exercise their ministry.

As long as the practice of religion is a freedom guaranteed by the Constitution, we are bound to have an enormous variety of religious practice. No authority external to religion can resolve the differences among religious groups or assure that they follow particular practices without threatening the religious freedom so important to our society. While churches cannot develop polities or practices that exempt them from such public-policy mandates as building codes or that allow them to treat employees less fairly than other employers, no one can interfere with their religious practices and beliefs.

If the only limitations on congregational autonomy can come from broader forms of church polity, and if such limitations are deemed unnecessary by local gatherings themselves, this completely autonomous type of religious group is likely to persist. It is an apparently inevitable corollary of religious freedom, and it exists at the opposite end of the spectrum from monarchical episcopacy.

RESOURCES ON CONGREGATIONS WITHOUT OVERSTRUCTURES

For Understanding Christian Churches (Disciples of Christ)

Adams, Hampton. *Why I Am a Disciple of Christ.* New York: Thomas Nelson and Sons, 1957.

Cartwright, Colbert S. *People of the Chalice: Disciples of Christ in Faith and Practice.* St. Louis: CBP Press, 1987.

Cummins, D. Duane. *A Handbook for Today's Disciples in the Christian Church (Disciples of Christ).* Rev. ed. St. Louis: Chalice Press, 1991.

The Design for the Christian Church (Disciples of Christ) and General Rules and Policies. Office of the General Minister and President. Indianapolis, n.d.

Duke, James O. *What Sort of Church Are We?* Council on Christian Unity, 1981.

Friedly, Robert L., and D. Duane Cummins. *The Search for Identity: Disciples of Christ—The Restructure Years, 1960–1985.* St. Louis: CBP Press, 1987.

McAllister, Lester G., and William E. Tucker. *Journey in Faith: A History of the Christian Church (Disciples of Christ).* St. Louis: Bethany Press, 1975.

Toulouse, Mark G. *Joined in Discipleship: The Shaping of Contemporary Disciples Identity.* St. Louis: Chalice Press, 1997.

Williams, D. Newell. *Ministry among Disciples: Past, Present, and Future.* Indianapolis and St. Louis: Council on Christian Unity, CBP Press, 1985.

————, ed. *A Case Study of Mainline Protestantism: The Disciples' Relation to American Culture, 1880–1989.* Grand Rapids, Mich.: Eerdmans; St. Louis: Chalice Press, 1991.

For Understanding Autonomous Congregations

Libby, Charles H. *Being Religious American Style: A History of Popular Religiosity in the United States.* Westport, Conn., and London: Greenwood Press, 1994.

Miller, Donald E. *Reinventing American Protestantism: Christianity in the New Millennium.* Berkeley: University of California Press, 1997.

Wagner, C. Peter, ed. *The New Apostolic Churches.* Ventura, Calif.: Regal Books, 1998.

Wuthnow, Robert. *The Restructuring of American Religion: Society and Faith since World War II.* Princeton, N.J.: Princeton University Press, 1988.

Epilogue

POLITIES AS LANGUAGES FOR DIALOGUE

T HE AIM OF THIS OVERVIEW has been simultaneously compre-
hensive and modest. Unless the overview is mistaken, the
options presented describe most, if not all, of the alternatives in
which Christians have given institutional form to their life together. There are, of course, many groups whose polities have not
been mentioned explicitly, but it is hoped that these groups will
find themselves identified with but minor variations as alternative
forms to one of the suggested models. Those interested can read
handbooks that attempt to be more complete in the discussion of
specific bodies, although the attention to governance in many of
those volumes is often subordinated to doctrine.

But the aim of this book has also been modest. It attempts to
render helpful descriptions rather than provide definitive evalu-
ations. No efforts have been made to adjudicate which form of
governance has the greatest biblical warrant or most adequately
embodies the Christian heritage. Such efforts have been made frequently throughout Christian history. Sometimes they have been
the chief focus of concern—often in polemical contexts. They are
still of interest as part of church history. Nor are such adjudi-
cations necessarily improper; in certain undertakings, they may
need due attention. But they differ from the modest agenda of
this work, which assumes that much can be gained from making
persons in one tradition aware of how different Christian groups
give institutional form to their central convictions. Such awareness can greatly enrich the understanding of one's own tradition
as well as provide insights into the approach of others.

A—perhaps *the*—traditional and customary way of looking at
polity is to view it as a form of law—church law. As such, polity

151

provides guidance for decision making and may even provide for the censure or ouster of those whose behavior does not accord with group standards. Law also provides the warrant or certification for official power. Despite the usefulness of seeing polity in how it directs a denomination, this way of viewing the subject can become the source of controversy and division when denominations have different readings of what the gospel requires.

To view polity as law is not necessarily adequate to understanding all of polity's functions or significance. Just as households are more than sets of rules, but consist of relationships involving trust and support, so ecclesial communities are served by polities that are more than procedural directives for maintaining proper order. Polities offer, not only rules for procedure, but models for interaction and fidelity.

It may be fruitful to think of polities as languages that facilitate interactions among group members. Thinking about polity in this way would shift the focus from what it prescribes to what is useful and supportive, procedurally helpful, and spiritually uplifting. Languages are as necessary, if not more so, for human interaction as laws. They are essential to practically every form of socialization or institutionalization. They create and sustain communities and give shape to the life of the persons who live in them. But they differ from laws.

In contrast to laws, which generally are assessed as correct or incorrect (or good or bad), languages are judged useful, facilitative, or functional. They may have aesthetic qualities of considerable significance. They make a difference in the culture and ethos of the communities that employ them, but they can differ from community to community without becoming occasions for conflict and hostility.

Laws judge behavior by setting standards frequently defended as valid in contrast to all alternatives. Languages can create community without a need to defend them as the only valid way of communicating. It is not necessary to reject or refute someone else's language. It is better to consider how languages should be understood and appreciated, if not shared. Whereas it is contradictory to embrace many legal systems at once, it is not impossible to embrace many languages. The more we know about other languages, the more we understand our own and the less inclined we are to insist that ours is the only valid way of speaking.

Languages are compatible with pluralism and diversity, yet they also make pluralism and diversity parts of a larger interchange. Cooperation is more feasible among communities of different languages than among jurisdictions of different laws. Although some have held that a common language is a prerequisite for unity among peoples, experience has shown that translations (whether conducted dialogically or simultaneously) make communication among different, even widely diverse, groups possible. Conversely, having one set of laws does not necessarily eliminate contentious debate.

For understanding to occur among communities with different languages, multilingual persons must interpret (that is, translate one language to another). Such persons may serve the interests of those speaking one language, but they must be fair in making others' statements as straightforward as they can. Diplomats do not expect translators or interpreters to preempt policy judgments.

What would it mean to treat ecclesiastical polities more like languages than laws? It would mean—at the most elemental level—that we would attempt to understand without rushing to judge whose governance is most correct. Such judgments might not need to be suspended entirely or forever, but they need to be subordinated to fair and open understanding. It is more important to understand polity as the language of others' households than to argue for polity as the law that everyone must obey.

Each of us recognizes that polity used as a means of exclusion (even if advanced for structured unity) has advocates. The argument, although made with sincere intentions, is based on a model of law and commitment with a long history in cultural settings of Christian churches. Theological forms of exclusion have developed as aspects of cultural exclusion, and vice versa. The consequence is generally to suggest that all Christians should submit to the laws of one household. It will not be easy to deconstruct these formulations or the attitudes that have fostered them. Some groups will find it easier to do this than others. But it is no more plausible to insist that a single polity is a precondition for Christian unity than to insist that a single language (identical vocabulary and grammar) must precede globalization. Ecclesial ecumenicity no more requires a single polity than international cooperation requires a single language. Unity does, however, require that polities be used with consistency, that they can be understood by others, and that they be openly espoused. There is no ecumenical promise in secretive societies.

The Bible supports both the idea that religious commitment must be singular and absolute and the legitimacy of diverse views. Perhaps the most vivid insistence on fidelity is the encounter on Mount Carmel between Elijah, the prophet of Yahweh, and the prophets of Baal (1 Kings 18:17–46). This story suggests that limping between opinions is unworthy, though it addresses loyalty to an Ultimate and does not settle all questions about religious institutions. But the Old Testament also contains material suggesting the legitimacy of more open and inclusive stances, such as the books of Ruth and Esther.

In the New Testament, we find words attributed to Jesus that support each approach. He said, "He who is not with me is against me" (Matthew 12:30), but elsewhere, "He that is not against us is for us" (Mark 9:40). One of the most difficult tasks of theology is to sort out when singular devotion is appropriate and when it is important to be open to other alternatives. It is legitimate to argue that, in our present situation, we need to wrestle with which of these approaches determines how we think about polity.

Several concordats in recent years provide for the mutual recognition of ministries of different denominations. These agreements effectively provide for "translations" among churches with different polities, without requiring organic unions. Lutherans and Episcopalians can now serve in each other's churches. The same is true of ministers in the Christian Churches (Disciples of Christ) and the United Church of Christ. Ministers of the Evangelical Lutheran Church in America, Presbyterian Church, Reformed Church in America, and United Church of Christ are reciprocally recognized by a Formula of Agreement drawn up in the late 1990s. The arrangements provide for cooperation based on a model of languages rather than a model of law. The polities (languages) are still different, but they are put to use for cooperation rather than division.

These agreements were made at the top level of the respective denominations. They will become most fruitful and significant, however, if ministers become aware of other polities that were party to the agreements and make a deliberate effort to understand both the similarities and differences among them. As they equip themselves to function as effective clergypersons in denominations with different polities, they can be the interpreters or translators who facilitate conversation. It is important that persons know the polities subject to the agreements and become knowledgeable about other polities, with whom further agreements may yet be made. Building an ecumenical household of faith may be more likely if individuals have made the effort to be at home in two or more polities, just as international cooperation is furthered by those who have become bilingual or multilingual. To become significant, compacts or covenants made at top levels require conversation partners at the lower levels.

Special arrangements are possible, according to some polities, for ministers to serve interdenominational parishes or to conduct special services outside the denominational structures, and still to maintain good standing within their own denomination. Moreover, in local practice, ministers of different denominations occasionally have celebrated the Eucharist together unofficially. There have been efforts in some circles to discourage this unofficial unity. Then, too, in denominations as a whole, some polity exclusivism has developed as a reaction to dissidents who have joined other ecclesial groups yet clung to their former membership. But the movement toward mutual recognition is stronger than the movement for legal purity.

Over recent years, seminary faculties have become interdenominational, even in many church-controlled institutions. Faculty members have often been picked for scholarly competence rather than denominational identity. There is currently a tendency to reverse this pattern and to staff seminaries only with faculty members of the sponsoring denomination. This tendency has arisen in part because scholars chosen for technical competence have not been diligent in becoming "multilingual" about polity. They have ignored (and at times disparaged) the polity of their home seminary's denomination rather than seeking to be partners in interpolity conversations. This means that one of the most potentially valuable aspects of faculty diversity has not always borne fruit. Theological inquiry among persons of diverse ecclesial identities can be especially valuable, but it must be carefully and deliberately cultivated by choosing persons who seek to be multilingual in their approach to church involvement.

Polity affects not only how churches govern their affairs and how they relate to each other as ecclesial institutions, but the stances they take in relationship to the world and its institutions. There are similarities and differences in how churches take such stances, as there are differences in their conduct of ecclesial affairs. Differences are evident regarding both social witness and personal behavior. Differences in both realms currently divide many churches, irrespective of their polity.

One view—generally associated with the view of polity as law—looks to church governance to provide authoritative guidance about ethical standards. Such a view is premised on a belief that agreement about polity could produce agreement about morality. Although this view has considerable history and still garners support, it is increasingly unsustainable. Even churches with the strongest sense of ecclesial authority as a function of polity find members making their own judgments about moral issues, both personal and social. Although this situation varies in substance and intensity from one religious group to another (or from one part of the world to another), it is clear that few, if any, religious groups of any size can expect their members to accept their teaching and to abide by their authoritative moral proclamations without question.

It may have been plausible at one time to think that churches could agree about moral matters even though they differed in beliefs about structure. But it seems that we no longer live in such circumstances. Not only do Christian groups differ about moral issues, they are frequently divided internally over such matters, on both denominational and congregational levels. Moreover, they are not having a great deal of success in resolving the disputes.

In an illuminating discussion of contemporary church life, Lewis Mudge considers the problems and promises that arise in efforts to initiate and sustain moral reflection in ecclesial communities. Aware of the present difficulties in pursuing this agenda, and aware of the deep divisions about moral issues in contemporary denominations, Mudge nevertheless holds that moral witness must be a central aspect of church life—an aspect that an ecumenical framework can greatly enhance. This is not because churches in the aggregate can offer moral answers, but because churches in ecumenical organizations gain space for moral explorations. The space opens from the requirement to interact with groups of diverse experiences and perspectives.

We, as Mudge frankly acknowledges, do not yet have such conversations (except in very rare circumstances, for a privileged few), but that need not preclude the mandate to seek them in a catholicity (universality) of inquiry and action through which the Spirit can work. Whether we are on the threshold of developing such processes in the Christian movement as a whole, or whether we are likely to see further decline in moral witness, is difficult to know. Mudge suggests:

> Ecumenism is a matter of ongoing learning through the experience of branches of the global household other than our own. We are called to a felt, experienced, and acted-out understanding of truth, righteousness, and peace in the global world (and perhaps cosmic) context of life, and thereby to contribute to the world's becoming one community under God.[1]

The possibility to which Mudge points will not come about by some grand strategy that—through either an intellectual or moral proclamation by a recognized authority—catapults unity into being. No polity will bring a common mind through institutional arrangements alone, nor will unity come without institutional embodiments. It will come more slowly, if it comes—incrementally and without fanfare, as Christians learn more about each other and realize that, while none of us has a monopoly on true faith or right practice, neither are we destined to a divisiveness that forever keeps Christians apart.

---

1. Lewis S. Mudge, *The Church as Moral Community: Ecclesiology and Ethics in Debate* (Geneva: WCC Publications; New York: Continuum, 1998), 148.

INDEX

classis, 67
clearness committee, 98
Committee on Ministry (Presbyterian), 69,
    71
competency, of members to govern. *See*
    soul competency
Conference Minister (President) in United
    Church of Christ, 124
conferences
    Episcopal, 24–25
    Methodist, 34–36
    United Church of Christ, 124
confirmation of new members
    Episcopal, 21
    Lutheran, 114
    Roman Catholic, 47
conflicts and disputers, 7–8, 76
Congregational Christian Churches, 122
congregational polities, differences, 9
congregationalism, R. W. Dales's principles
    of, 120
congregations
    conferencing between, in Mennonite
        polity, 92
    See also local congregations
Conservative Congregational Christian
    Conference, 123n
Consistory, 71
Constantelos, Demetrios J., 58
constitutions, 2–5, 45
    amending of, 72
Consultation on Church Union (COCU),
    x–xi
covenants of purpose, 122–23
creeds, place of, 1–2, 104. *See also* Book of
    Confessions

Dale, R. W., 120n
deacons, diaconate
    Christian (Disciples of Christ), 143
    Church of Jesus Christ of LDS, 80
    Episcopal, 47–48
    Lutheran, 107
    Mennonite, 89, 93–94
    Methodist, 34
    Orthodox, 58

Presbyterian, 65
    United Church of Christ, 123
    See also permanent diaconate
Directory of Worship, Presbyterian, 76
discernment, 95–97
discipline of members
    in Amish groups, 91–92
    in Society of Friends, 97–98
district superintendents, 38
Dordrecht Confession of Faith, 89, 91

ecumenical councils, 25–26
ecumenicity, 38, 115–6, 157. *See also*
    Consultation on Church Union
elders, 8, 116
    differences between churches, 9
    Christian (Disciples of Christ), 142–43
    Church of Jesus Christ LDS, 80, 83
    Hutterite, 90
    Lutheran, 107, 109
    Methodist, 34
    Presbyterian, 64–65, 67, 68, 69, 74
    ruling, 64
    Society of Friends, 95–96
    teaching, 64
enforcement of rules of polity, 7
England, Church of, 66
Enlightenment, idea of liberty in, 140
episcopacy, 8
    differences between churches, 9
    exemplary, 57–59
    managerial, 28–42
    monarchical, 13–27
    pastoral, 43–56
    See also bishops
Episcopal Church, 9, 43–56, 154
establishment, political, of religion, 66
Eucharist, 6, 54, 155. *See also* Lord's
    Supper
Evangelical and Reformed Church, 122
Evangelical Lutheran Church in America,
    112–14
exclusion, polity as an instrument of, 153
Executive (or General) Presbyter, 70